MEMORIES

of

DARLINGTON

2

Dorothy,

Many thanks for your help,

Chris Lloyd

Cover Design by Greg Marshall
Cover pictures: Tubwell Row in 1900, Prebend Row in the 1890s
© **The Northern Echo**

Introduction

THIS is the second Memories of Darlington book which is something of a 'greatest hits' from my weekly local history column in The Northern Echo. The column doesn't set out to be a boring history textbook crammed with dates. It is about the buildings and the people who lived in them. It is about anecdotes and memories which even those with just a passing interest in Darlington will find entertaining.

The environment, the history, the stories, the characters and the memories are the things which shape modern life. This book is a selection of them....

Acknowledgements

FROM the supreme Victorian chronicler William Longstaffe to his modern contemporaries George Flynn and Vera Chapman, taking in over the decades the anonymous reporters of the local newspapers – The Northern Echo, Darlington and Stockton Times, Northern Despatch and North Star – this book has sources too numerous to list.

Special thanks must go to the staff of Darlington's Centre for Local Studies – Kimberley Bennett, Margaret White, Gillan Wilson, Brian Myers, Katherine Williamson and Alyson Herbert – who rarely failed in pointing me in the direction of the above sources.

Thanks also to The Northern Echo's photographers who never failed to complain about copying decaying pictures, to James Espin for finally believing in this project, to Stan Dean for checking it out, to Sue Kendrew for laying it out and to Greg Marshall for his design work. But most importantly, enormous thanks to anyone who ever read, wrote or called. **Chris Lloyd**

Photographs

'Darlington Today' photographs by Nigel Whitfield. Archive photographs courtesy of Arts, Libraries and Museums Department, Durham County Council

CONTENTS

WATERING HOLES

WELLS AND FOUNTAINS

FROM time immemorial drinking water came from a dirty little hole in the ground. Pigs and cattle trampled around the well-head, and the street was strewn with human rubbish. Hygiene was not an over-riding consideration. The first mention of a well in the annals of Darlington comes in 1309 and it is to 'a venell called Hundgate Well' which was probably situated towards the Feethams end of that street.

Two centuries later and le Tubbwell had taken pre-eminence for when in 1545 the town is referred to as 'Darneton upon the well', the well in question is that in Tubwell Row. Until 1760, such was the importance of the well that it, and its fellow in Skinnergate, had two full-time overseers ensuring no-one tampered with the contents.

The seriousness of such a crime is best shown by the severity of punishment. The Borough Books of 1612 order:

'None shall wash cloathes, fish, or such like things at the Tubwell to putrifie the same upon paine of 6s 8d' – a substantial amount of money'.

Until 1846 the wells were Darlington's main source of water; the Skerne was little more than a stinking open sewer. Many enterprising householders collected rain in butts, but these were never washed out. When in 1851 a doctor supervised the cleaning of a butt in a yard in Bondgate he was horrified to discover at the bottom a decomposing body of a baby. For a month the inhabitants of the yard had been blithely drinking the water, oblivious to the source of its piquant flavour. But then, Darlingtonians may have been accustomed to their tea having a human taste. Skinnergate well (on the Duke Street side of the road opposite Mechanics Yard) was lined with rough-hewn, ill-fitting stones and sunk in sand.

Tubwell Row, 1890, with le Tubbwell in the centre of the picture with a pump on it. In the 1990s, the wide sweep of the pavement has been reconstructed to mirror the old days. Left, Tubwell Row as it is today.

Therefore, particularly when a pump was installed (pumps probably came in the 1830s and 1840s), water would be sucked in from all sides.

And what is worryingly close to the well? The Friends Burial Ground, which is also on sandy soil so easing drainage.

This was one of the prime reasons given for the closure of Skinnergate well in 1885. The same council meeting decided the Tubwell was also too contaminated to remain, but it continued as a source until another meeting in 1898. Then an analyst condemned its waters as 'absolutely unfit for drinking purposes', and they undoubtedly contained 'sewage materials'.

The closure of the wells did not cause a drought in Darlington. On

Wednesday, April 24 1850, the town was awash with the news that a new, cleaner brand of water was being introduced from the Broken Scar water-works. Edward Pease wrote:

> *'There was considerable stir in Darlington today, this being the first day water was brought into the town from the New Water Works.'*

However, there was a great deal of scepticism about the benefits of Tees water, particularly as farmers believed cows that had grazed by the riverside contracted a lung disease. But once the new water had tickled the towns-peoples' tastebuds they took to it like the proverbial duck. The real clinch-er was that it made better tea and beer than the pump muck.

To encourage the population to drink clean water the Local Government Board decided to use fountains as advertisements. The Board bought the waterworks in 1854 and on August 4, 1856 commissioned town surveyor, Mr G Mason, to design and build the first advert for the top of Tubwell Row.

THE TUBWELL TORRENTOR

IT was designed as an animal fountain for the herds of beasts that sauntered around town on market day. Sadly, when Mr Mason's marvellous edifice arrived in May 1857 it was discovered that the basin which had been pre-pared for it was far too small. So Mason's masterpiece had to be transferred to the centre of Bondgate.

The Board cast around for a replacement, hit upon the Tubwell Tor-rentor and struck upon great trouble. Darlington lacked a proper drainage system. The water gushed out of the Tubwell Torrentor and poured down the road, turning Tubwell Row into a muddy dung-track in hottest summer, and a skating dung-rink in coldest winter.

Farmers feared that diseased swine, horses or cattle would pass on infections to clean beasts while drinking in the fountain trough.

So the town elders decided the Tubwell Torrentor was not a good idea. Joseph Pease of Southend volunteered to take it and put it in the farthest part of his garden that is now South Park.

But the water pressure down by the Skerne wasn't great enough, so the fountain was placed beside the boating lake behind Harewood Hill. Despite the passing of the Peases and the ravaging (however genteely) of the Southend Estate Company which built on Joseph's gardens, the fountain stood steadfast.

The little lake beside it was filled in, the boathouse opposite it was lovingly converted into Avenue Cottage, and then, in 1960, the area surrounding it was given to the town from the estate of Dr John Waldy as Green Park. At that time the Darlington and Stockton Times described the Torrentor as 15ft across and 12ft high,

A contemporary drawing of the Tubwell Torrentor – which has the people way out of scale.

'A pair of up-turned dolphins form part of the top and these in turn support a pair of cherubs rather the worse for wear holding aloft a jet from which water once issued'.

It remained in Green Park until the 1970s when it was replaced by the children's swings. The Torrentor moved back to the town centre, to Bull Wynd on the corner of Houndgate.

Sadly, it no longer holds pride of place. The dolphins and cherubs were in such a poor state of repair they were removed and it now sits on its third pedestal. The plaque telling the world of its 140-year history has been torn off; cigarette packets fill the trough from which in its heyday animals drank their fill, but at least in early 1995 it received a coat of paint.

THE FOTHERGILL FOUNTAIN

THE Local Government Board wanted fountains to spring up all over town to promote the use of clean water. Darlington Temperance Society wanted a proliferation of fonts to provide an alternative to foul alcohol.

Early in the last century Darlington was awash with drink. Children were pumped full of beer and wine at social 'dos'; doctors freely prescribed alcoholic liquors, and society regarded reaching the state of drunkenness as a great achievement. The Americans thought otherwise and dreamt up the the idea of a Temperance Society. It caught on in Britain in 1830 when the Seven Men of Preston signed the pledge and set the trend. One of the seven, Richard Turner, had a terrible stammer (not withdrawal symptoms). He said nothing but being 'te-te-total' would satisfy him, and a new word entered the English language.

South Park, Darlington

Top left: the opening ceremony of Fothergill's Fountain, June 10, 1862. Botton leftt: The Fothergill Fountain in South Park after 1880. Right: Postcard commemorating the opening of the Temperance Institute in Gladstone Street on September 23, 1903.

Opened by The Earl of Carlisle, Sept. 23rd, 1903, at a cost of over £5,000.

DARLINGTON TEMPERANCE INSTITUTE

One of the first teetotal groups in the country started in Darlington in 1831. It was called the Moderation Society, and George Mottram was an early convert. He was an original drunken sailor and was condemned to death for stealing a boat. On renouncing alcohol he was pardoned and set sail for Darlington where he became a leading light in the Society.

One day he cast off for Barnard Castle to address a meeting, but got so hopelessly drunk on the journey he was unable to speak on his arrival. Mortified by the twist in his sobriety, George decided to go the whole hog and join the Total Abstinence Society.

Within 12 months the Moderation movement had collapsed and in 1835 the abstainers re-grouped under the banner of Total Abstinence. In turn this evolved into the Temperance Society, and the first meetings were held in a watchmaker's shop in High Row.

In these early days Temperance was greeted with cynicism. The established church believed teetotalism was taking the place of God and was carried out in an un-Christian spirit. In Darlington the Wesleyans sacked a Sunday school teacher when he became a 'Temp' because of his new movement's 'erroneous teachings'.

But the Society prospered although at its 1852 annual public tea – it could hardly hold a cheese and wine party – members were saddened by the numbers that had fallen from grace once the hay and corn harvests had been collected.

And so it looked to ways of spreading its message. In 1860, it sponsored drinking cups which were fitted to Darlington's fountains, and then it began plotting its coup de grace.

It asked the Local Government Board if it could build a fountain of its very own in Prospect Place to tempt the tipplers away from the demon drink. The Board refused on the grounds that the fountain would be a traffic hazard (as Joseph Pease's statue was when it was placed in Prospect Place in 1875).

Undeterred, in July 1861 the Society got word that the Board was going to replace the Bondgate Bubbler – Mr Mason's original fountain from Tubwell Row which was now turning another part of town into a mire. Once the Bondgate Bubbler was pensioned off to Cleveland Lodge in Great Ayton, the home of John Pease, a fountain-designing competition was organised by the Society.

Septimus Hird won the two-guinea top prize. Aged 17, Septimus lived, ironically, in the Green Tree Inn, Skinnergate. Before his stout design left the drawing board, Septimus drowned while bathing at Redcar – an obelisk was erected in his memory in West Cemetery.

Septimus's fountain was also a memorial. It was dedicated to Dr John Fothergill, a man born in Wensleydale who was elected the first president of the Society by those gathered in the watchmaker's shop in 1835. He held that post until his death in 1858.

On Tuesday June 10, 1862 the Temps gathered at the Mechanics Institute and processed to the fountain in the middle of Bondgate. William Thompson, Fothergill's successor as president, drunk the first glass of water and declared the fountain open.

But, naturally enough, the Fothergill Fountain had the same bad effect as the Bondgate Bubbler and the Tubwell Torrentor. A raised pedestrian crossing had to be built from Skinnergate to North Bondgate so people did not get their shoes dirty.

For the Railway Jubilee in 1875 it was decided to remove the fountain altogether, and South Park became its home. With the gas disconnected, the light on top of the canopy was replaced in 1880 by a stone bowl donated by a Mr Ross.

However, the Temperance Society was thriving. In 1881, the leader of the Blue Ribbon Mission came to town and it was estimated that a quarter of the 32,000 population were 'blue-ribboners', or had taken the pledge.

At the speechifying, Darlington Temps boasted that the Highland Laddie had become a temperance hall; the Royal Oak a bootmaker's; the Dun Cow a solicitor's office and the Talbot a shoe emporium.

On a roll, finances were accumulated for a Temperance Institute, and a foundation stone was laid in Gladstone Street in July 1902. Fourteen months later the £5,000 Institute opened for business with, said the Darlington and Stockton Times, 'up to date furnishings and electrical arrangements, not omitting the penny-in-the-slot telephone'. The reporter also noted that the Institute's kitchen would be connected to all rooms by a 'metraphone'.

The Institute's attractions included a billiard room and a bathroom where a hot or cold shower cost 4d, and quickly proved so popular the building was overwhelmed. In September 1909 a £2,000 Temperance Hall was founded next door, and it was opened in February 1910 by Mr EB Mounsey.

He said 'it would tend to make men, women and children happier, better and more Christ-like'. For a while the 600-seater Hall was fully-utilised. More than 50 trade unions and friendly societies met inside.

The heady days of abstinence lasted a couple of decades. In 1946 when Charles Simon's Repertory Company occupied the Hall it burnt down, and the Temps never had funds to restore it.

The popular advent of television kept many members at home. In September 1957 the Gladstone Street buildings were put up for sale; in 1958 the Temps moved out, and in 1959 the Hall was demolished and the Institute converted into shops.

The plaque on the front of the Temperance Institute can still be seen in Gladstone Street and the Fothergill Fountain next to the aviary in South Park still bears witness to the first president.

THE GUSHER ON THE GREEN

THE RED granite fountain that stands proudly among the flowers in the middle of Cockerton Green was originally in Stanwick Park on the estate of the Duke of Northumberland, and so its early history is unknown.

The Stanwick sprinkler officially became the gusher on the green on August 1, 1924 when the mayoress, Mrs R Loraine, turned on the water. It was a present to the village from Coun Sutherland, but many people regarded it is a sop.

Cockerton lost its individual council in 1915 when it was swallowed up by Darlington Corporation. The Corporation promised much – many great gifts to improve the quality of life – but delivered little: a single fountain.

And it was a fountain that could hardly raise a trickle. Within a couple of decades the council planted some flowers in the basin. The railings were removed in the early-1940s to assist the War Effort.

Left: The fountain on Cockerton Green pictured in 1956. Below: The Pierremont Vase in full glory on Henry Pease's estate, Pierremont Mansion. This picture was taken before 1900

THE PIERREMONT VASE

DARLINGTON'S most impressive fountain is The Pierremont Vase which now stands in South Park, a shadow of its former itself. It dates from some time after 1864 when Henry Pease turned his attention to the gardens of the Pierremont mansion he had bought in 1846.

Pierremont – originally named Pierpont and, amazingly, translated as 'the house on the hill overlooking the Cocker Beck' – was built in the 1830s off Woodland Road on the town's manure dump by John Botcherby. He swore it would be the grandest villa in town and that the Peases would never own it – it only became the grandest villa when Henry moved in.

The Pierremont Vase stands 20 ft tall. It was set beside an ornamental lake which was decorated by tumbling rocks, an island grotto and a water-fall, all lit by gas lamps. It had 21 jets of water, and a main basin surrounded by 12 flower vases on pillars. It was edged by semi-circular flower beds. However, the whole Pierremont experience was far too large for a modern family, and when Henry's second wife Mary, who outlived him by 28 years, died in 1909 the estate was gradually sold off for housing. At a rough guess, Pierremont Gardens today stands where the real gardens of Pierremont used to be.

It is quite ironic that the most famous monument to Henry Pease should be a fountain, for he was one of the original shareholders in the Darlington Water Company that was responsible for providing the town with a main supply in the early 1850s. It is recorded that when the Local Government Board assumed control of the town's waterworks in 1854, Henry was most upset.

Builder and councillor Cuthbert Joseph Todd presented The Pierremont Vase to the town in July 1925 as the plaque on the fountain base still notes. For a while it preserved some of its former glory in South Park, but now it has suffered a fate common to most of Darlington's fountains and been relegated to a forgotten corner.

MURAL FOUNTAINS

A TRICKLE of an idea came into Joseph Pease's head in 1865. He had just developed the 'mural fountain' concept, and stuck the first one on the wall by the entrance to his mansion in Grange Road. He thought: 'Perhaps Darlington would like a complete set.'

So in March 1866 he offered eight to the town and the Local Government Board agreed to lay on free water. Only three of the nine mural (or wall) drinking fountains still exist and the precise sites of several of the others are not known. All founts in the wall were built on the boundaries of properties belonging to the Pease family. The most ornate spouters were in Woodland Road (extant) and Carmel Road (disappeared since the 1950s). The surrounding carved stonework contained the date, and in the middle were metal panels displaying a dolphin with bullrushes.

Over the dolphin's head hung a trident which obviously has connections with Neptune, the King of the Waters. In the middle at the top was the Pease family crest: a dove rising with a pea stalk in its beak. The metalwork also bore the legend 'water for the thirsty'.

The other founts in the wall were not so elaborate. They were situated in Coniscliffe Road (extant), Northgate, North Road (both appear to have disappeared since the 1950s), near the gateway to the East Mount mansion in Haughton Road (disappeared when East Mount was demolished after the Second World War), and two were placed at either end of the Bank Top Cut (vanished when the cut was widened in the 1930s).

THE FINAL FOUNTAIN

THE supply of fountains has all but dried up. Only one has escaped, but that is because there is hardly a drop of history to accompany it.

It stands in South Park and in 1991 had to be skilfully repaired after vandals gave it a good kicking. Nowadays it acts as a pretty flowerbowl.

The final fountain once stood by a pond on the west side of Beechwood Avenue on the Southend estate. It probably dates from the late-1860s and would have come into the town's possession when the estate was being dismantled at the turn of the century.

BOTTLED WATER

A CENTURY ago Darlington had six or seven mineral water manufacturers, the largest of which was Darlington Bottling and Mineral Water Company in Gladstone Street which lasted long enough to celebrate its 50th anniversary in 1939. Other notables included Charles H Wren on Bank Top and James Swenden. Initially Charles Wren – whose middle-name is given variously as Henry and Herbert – called his operation The Darlington Aerated Water Company, and it first comes to the notice of historians with an advert in the Darlington and Stockton Times on July 9, 1881. This publicised his 'potash water, lemonade and ginger ale' which sold at 1s 6d a dozen.

James Swenden was originally a chemist and worked in London in a pharmaceutical enterprise selling to literary giants like Dickens and Thackeray. In Darlington he set up as a chemist but sold out to Hodgson's in 1894 so he could begin as a mineral water bottler behind in Buckton's Yard. Swenden died in 1909 although his company lasted until 1955 when it was one of the last in its field to close.

All of these companies churned out 'Codd's bottles' embossed with their names. The bottles were named after inventor Hiram Codd in 1875.

James Swenden, bottled water manufacturer

The gas within the lemonade or aerated water would rise and so force the marble against the neck, thus preventing the fizz from escaping. However, Victorian children preferred playing marbles to collecting bottles and so smashed the neck to get the marble out – hence the word 'codds-wallop' for once broken a bottle is indeed a load of codswallop.

BREWING

THE heyday of the water bottling industry coincided with a time when Darlington had at least three breweries. Way back when, every publican would have brewed his own ale. Well, actually it normally was his wife who did the hard work and so today's licensing sittings are called Brewster Sessions – brewster being the female equivalent of brewer. Perhaps it was the Quaker influence but Darlington is unusual in that it didn't have a large brewery until late in the last century and even that – the Darlington Brewery Co – was financially unsuccessful and was wound up in 1881. All but three of the small pub-based breweries from this time floundered, and these three were taken over by businessmen with the necessary cash. Haughton Road Brewery was probably the biggest of them all. Initially it was based in two small cottages next to the Havelock pub and called itself the South Durham Brewery Co. All this changed when solicitor Thomas Clayhills (the legal family firm still exists) bought and completely rebuilt the premises in 1894. His water came from a specially-sunk 260ft Artesian

A Codd's Bottle embossed with the name of Haughton Road Brewery – it would have been a water bottle, though, because beer was flat and so didn't need to be in an expensive Codd's

Well. It was pumped up to the top of the brewery, pumped down to ground-level for the fermentation process, pumped back to the top where the liquor was cooled in the breeze, and then finally pumped back down to the ground for barrelling.

Since 1885 Clayhills had been collecting pubs in Darlington – his first acquisitions were the Hope Inn, Yarm Road, and the Three Crowns, Archer Street – and the takeover of Haughton Road Brewery made sound centralising sense. Clayhills' final pub purchase was the Travellers Rest at Cockerton which he totally rebuilt in 1925 so Auckland Road could be widened. When his son, Thomas Clayhills-Henderson who had taken over the business on his death, died in 1933 the family owned 41 pubs and 11 off-licences. The following year the pubs and the brewery were sold for £82,000 to the John Smith Tadcaster Brewery Co, and brewing immediately ceased. Those Darlington pubs which transferred to Smith's included the three mentioned above plus the Dolphin Hotel, Market Place; Golden Cock, Tubwell Row; Grey Horse, Bank Top; Grey Horse Inn, Haughton; Curriers Arms, Commercial Street; Baydale Beck; Fighting Cocks, Middleton St. George, and the Foresters at Coatham Mundeville. Four years earlier Smith's had made a similar swoop in Darlington for Hinde's Brewery and its 14 inns – this explains why the town has a preponderance of Smith's pubs not found elsewhere in the North-East.

Hinde's was founded in 1871 in Ridsdale Street by Thomas Perkin Hinde and his brother George Ridsdale Hinde. TP Hinde sounds a remarkable character. His father was landlord at the Waterloo Hotel, and TP's first job was in the 1850s in the telegraph service in York. One day he overslept and failed to telegraph to northern newspapers the vital news that Britain had concluded peace with Russia following the Crimean War. Rather than face demotion, TP resigned and with his brother GR emigrated to New Zealand. They joined the army, fought the natives, narrowly escaped an ambush and returned to Darlington to build the Eastbourne Brewery.

They stuck the brewery business for four years before selling up and moving to California. There they became fruit-growers and wine-producers before TP noticed in a paper from back home (both the Darlington and Stockton Times and the North Star claimed credit) that Eastbourne Brewery had failed and was up for sale again.

So in 1885 the Hinde brothers were back in Darlington and brewing. They renamed their works the National Brewery and passed it on to TP's son, Thomas Morton Hinde who became Darlington mayor in 1921. A few years after TM's death, John Smith's made an offer and brewing stopped.

The third Darlington brewery, Warwick's Victoria Brewery in Fry Street and I'Anson Street in Rise Carr and Haughton Road, succumbed to the lure of money even earlier than Hinde's. Henry Warwick bought the Victoria from ex-mayor Edward Manners in 1888. Upon his death in 1900 the eldest of his children, Ernest, took charge. However, in the 1920s, Ernest's epilepsy worsened, he retired and the North-Eastern Brewery Company – later Vaux – stepped in. Ernest died in 1926 – 'suicide while temporarily insane', concluded the Coroner.

BEFORE THE CORNMILL

O N August 27, 1992, the largest construction job in Darlington town centre this century opened for business. The developers of the Cornmill Shopping Centre may have had a firm grasp on building matters, but their grasp on history was a tad wayward.

Wayward by only a few yards, though, for the true Corn Mill was on the other side of Crown Street where today there is a rutted car park. A thousand years ago, the bishops who ruled County Durham had an oppressive monopoly on corn-grinding in Darlington. Everyone was compelled to use their mills and, through the miller, they took their cut: one-sixteenth of the corn if the miller had to deliver it; one-thirty-second if the corn-owner did the carrying.

In Darlington the main mill was in Lower Priestgate. A large Mill Pot was created where today's car park is and the Corn Mill was situated a little to the south of Priestgate.

It was the Mill Pot that made Darlington so unhealthy, particularly in summer, for as the flow of the Skerne slowed, so all the sewage and debris collected in the Pot which became stagnant, green and smelly. Very early records refer to the 'lingering' stream which formed a 'pool and morass' from opposite the church to the mill.

Gradually as the dominance of the bishops decreased, the monopoly lapsed, and merchants took over the mills. Growing up in Darlington in the 16th Century was a woollen industry which by the 18th Century had made the town renowned for its 'huckaback' – linen used for towels and tablecloths. In the early 1700s one of the leading woollen merchants was Joseph Coldwell. He bought wool from farmers, and then farmed it out to cottage industries to be washed, combed and spun. Joseph had a daughter who married Joseph Pease (1665-1719) of Shafton, York, and the young couple set about creating a dynasty.

Pease's Mill, Lower Priestgate, 1970: here was the Corn Mill in ancient times. This is now the site of the NCP car park.

Their son was Edward (1711-1785) who in 1744 moved to Darlington to take over the Coldwell family wool business. Towards the end of the century, with the Industrial Revolution setting in, the Peases moved into factories and in 1781 Joseph (1737-1808) bought the Corn Mill, leather mill and bark mill off Priestgate for £890. By 1824 the Revolution was complete: working from home was finished; everyone was in the water-powered mill.

Another revolution was starting, though. Here in the newly-acquired mill offices, Joseph's son Edward (1767-1858) drew up the prospectuses for the Stockton to Darlington Railway. For the Pease family had prospered: as woollen merchants they had looked at ways of making payment easier and had set up their own bank. Now, as men of money, inventors with madcap ideas, like George Stephenson, approached them for backing.

Priestgate Mill also thrived, its premises expanding over the Mill Holme. And upwards, too, in 1873-4 with the building of the 152ft landmark chimney. Although the Peases prided themselves on using the most modern power source, the chimney was built (on shifting sands, incidentally, as centuries ago the meandering Skerne stretched from Crown Street to the Ford garage) by donkey-power. The 395,000 bricks were attached to a pulley, and as a tied-on donkey was led up Priestgate, so the bricks were winched to the top. It must have taken a lot of carrots.

The advent of the tower showed the permanency of steam-power, which meant the old water-wheels could go. Filling in the Mill Pot began, and with-

Left: The second Priestgate mill in 1870 where the MFI car park is today. Right: February 26, 1894, the day of Darlington's biggest fire. The entire central section of Pease's Mill has collapsed

in a few years enough land had been reclaimed from the Skerne for industrial Crown Street to be built.

Then, shortly before noon on February 26, 1894, what is possibly Darlington's biggest fire struck, doing £20,000 worth of damage. Ten floors of spinning machinery toppled in on one another.

'The walls rocked, and clouds of smoke rose in the air, and when the thunder-like noise had somewhat ceased, the dreadful nature of the ruin caused by the flames was evidenced in the mass of debris in an unshapely mass laying piled at the bottom of the gaunt, blackened walls,'

wrote a Darlington and Stockton Times reporter who was probably related to Shakespeare.

But like the proverbial phoenix, Pease's Mill re-emerged. During the Second World War mill workers produced yarn for half-a-million soldiers' battle dress – the thread for the yarn would have spun around the world 300 times. The post-War financial climate was not beneficial to this old industry, and in the 1960s the newer mill on East Street was demolished to make way for a ten-pin bowling alley which has since become MFI and Club Lucys. The Crown Street mill clung on, despite closing for business in 1972, until the 1980s. When the landmark chimney was felled in a cloud of dust in June 1984 it was clear that the manufacturing era of the Corn Mill had been overtaken by the consumerist era of the Cornmill.

But what else did Darlington lose to the consumerist era when the Cornmill was built?

Milbank, the corner between Tubwell Row and Crown Street , demolished 1850

CROWN STREET

THIS part of town started life as a narrow yard called Mill Hill, Mill Entry or plain Milbank (usually with just one 'l' in the middle). The entrance was off Priestgate, and the Corn Mill and the River Skerne were on the east side with a mix of industry and homes on the west. As it neared Tubwell Row it became narrower, and on the edge of the Mill Pot another row of hovels clung precariously.

Last century the Skerne had a propensity to flood in winter, and so those bankside houses must have been damp to say the least. The floods even claimed a victim: Henry Nesbitt, commonly known as Harry Boots. He was the mail cart conductor and on November 26, 1846 he decided to cut along through the flooded Milbank to reach the Post Office in Northgate. He never made it. Other posties came that night and pulled his up-turned cart and horses out of the Mill Pot, but they couldn't find Harry. They even tried the old wives' trick of bread with quicksilver (mercury) on it cast onto the water's surface. It was said the loaf would come to rest above the body. It didn't. It just circled round and round in the swirling current, and disappeared. But perhaps poor old Harry was doing the same.

The next morning his body was spotted, going round and round in the current until someone pulled him out. He was buried in St Cuthbert's churchyard. The dilapidated houses of Milbank were bought by the Board of Health in the early-1850s with the idea in mind of building a new, healthy street. An 1854 medical officer's report on the state of the Milbank area makes unsanitary reading:

'Dysentery, diarrhoea and fever have broken out among the dirty, ragged Irish creatures who are existing in the low, crowded and ill-ventilated hovels. Unless steps are taken to remove the abominable pig-sties and open dung hills, together with a free use of whitewash to purify these abodes of squalor, poverty and wretchedness, the malaria generated here must spread and taint the whole neighbourhood.'

The officer added, almost as an after thought:

'A slaughterhouse is here and the offal gets thrown onto the open dung hill.'

There's another tale that deserves to be told before it is lost forever along with Milbank. On a dark winter night in the 1780s, a youth was standing on a corner of one of the passages which led from Tubwell Row through to the Mill Entry behind. He was, by all accounts, on an 'assignation' keeping a watch on all that went on in the Row from which he was concealed by the shadows. A door beside him suddenly burst open. A man came out and deliberately placed a stool on the pavement and then returned inside. The man re-emerged carrying a hammer, a shepherd's crook and a lighted candle. Standing on the stool he banged the crook into one of the passageway's beams. Then he dismounted, went inside and returned bearing a rope. He carefully looped it over the protuding crook, tested its strength with a couple of trial pulls, put his neck in the noose, kicked his stool from under him and launched himself into eternity. Having seen enough, the watching youth sauntered off home.

Next morning a commotion broke out in Tubwell Row. Suicide! Suicide! People gathered on corners to discuss the sensation. One gaggle of gossips couldn't believe the news, until a passing youth casually said: "'Tis true enough. I saw him do it.' As the youth lost his youth and became an old man, someone asked why on that winter night, he had done nothing to prevent the man committing the ultimate sin. The reply was characteristically casual. 'Nay, nay,' he said. 'I thought he had the right to please himself.'

Strange behaviour. Equally strange was that someone took the trouble to sketch this unpicturesque stretch before it was pulled down in 1866. In the 1870s, the Mill Pot was filled in and so there was enough room to build a new street – Crown Street – which in 1891 was connected up to Northgate. However, it wasn't until the very late 1890s that they got around to building the warehouses which shield the brickwork of the Cornmill complex from open view.

The view down Tubwell Row in 1900

TUBWELL ROW

SOME evil spirit from the depths of hell must have infested Darlington planning department in the 1960s. It seemed determined to rip the very heart out of the town, to produce buildings with no character, to destroy the souls of the people who lived, worked and shopped there.

At least the Cornmill has exorcised much of that evil spirit's work – whatever you may feel about the replacement buildings. Admittedly Tubwell Row has never been an oil painting, but the ravages of the past have left it with just two buildings thought by the Department of the Environment worthy of preserving for posterity.

One of the greatest abominations – but by no means *the* greatest – was the thoughtless glass and perspex slabs of the late-1960s Barclays Bank at the bottom of Tubwell Row. It replaced some heavy-looking former houses from the back end of the last century. The shops at the very foot of Tubwell Row appear to date back to the demolition of Milbank, with the light brick building (currently an art gallery) a saleroom in its original incarnation.

Underneath it was the entrance to Greenup's Yard which stood on the eastern most bank of the Skerne's old course. In the 17th Century these properties were known as Cherry Garth until, in the 1860s, grocer Mr Greenup took over shop fronting Tubwell Row.

Left: The horrible 1960s architecture of Tubwell Row – Barclays Bank and the Co-Op. Below: A general view of Tubwell Row in the 1950s, before any building work started

The most memorable inhabitant of the yard was Richard Merryweather, a churchwarden. In 1760 he was fined 6d 'for laying his dunghill in the streets of the borough'. A couple of doors down from Greenup's Yard was Dryden's Yard (an entrance to it survived beside Barclay's Bank until the bank was demolished in the late-1980s). The buildings in the yard were pulled down in 1960.

William Dryden, a painter and decorator, had his shop front on Tubwell Row in the last half of the last century but, as with Greenup's Yard, the most interesting character in Dryden's Yard was not the man whose name it bore. That honour fell to Thomas Reed, the man who in the early part of the 19th Century was the setter-up of the market sheep pens. In his spare time he

The Raby Hotel, on the right of the picture, in the 1890s

washed sheep and fleeces in the Skerne, but Thomas himself was not a leading practitioner in the art of cleanliness. An 1856 book recalls:

> *'Tom had no great love for water as beverage, and was a narrow economist in its use for personal ablutions. The wettings which he incidentally received while sheep-plunging were to him a sufficient application of the pure element, and the complexion of his countenance a matter of perfect indifference.'*

In clean English, he smelt and couldn't care less.

But even Tommy Reed's odour would have been overpowered by the evil spirit which infested his neighbourhood with its biggest abomination: the twin 'loudspeakers' of the Darlington Co-operative Society that deafeningly dwarfed the poor Raby Hotel.

The Raby began life about 250 years ago as the Pack Horse Inn. It changed its name in 1874 to pay tribute to the family that had once owned it. Probably this was the time when the inn was rebuilt, expanding eastwards over Rebecca White's Yard. Out the back the Raby had its own yard which contained a couple of houses and was where on a Monday geese were driven for sale and slaughter.

During the late-1950s the Co-op cast covetous eyes at the Hotel because it was the only property in this stretch of Tubwell Row it had been unable to buy since 1930. The brewery stood strong and so DCS built around the pub, covering over Crabtree Yard to the west, Raby and Robinson's Yards to the east. The Raby lived out its last decade from 1976 as the Pied Piper when it and, thankfully, the DCS buildings were demolished to make way for the Cornmill. Laid to rest with the pub was a ghost reputed to haunt its upstairs rooms, and the last closet-bed in town.

Closet-beds were once very popular. They were built in a recess off the bar, separated by a curtain or double doors from the serving area. Presumably people who had been served too much were able to sleep off their stupor in the conveniently close closet-bed.

Perhaps they would have been better to slip outside, for just a few yards up from the Raby was the Tub Well. It was outside Davison's Yard (unofficially called Tann Yard as at the bottom there was a large tannery) which fronted Tubwell Row with a saw-pit. Even today, the pump handle marking the site of the well is substantially higher than the road: a large lay-by was cut into this bank so the top of wagons delivering to the yard were at pavement height.

Because Tubwell Row has been so troubled by builders, the street has only two listed buildings. The first is the Golden Cock which lost its 17th Century outbuilding – constructed with 'random rubble and old bricks' according to the Department of the Environment – to the voracious Cornmill.

Three hundred years or so ago the inn on this site was known as the Blue Boar. It then became the Three Jolly Travellers and changed name again in 1762 to the Boot and Slipper. On July 11, 1823 the house-cum-school to the east of the Boot and Slipper began shaking.

An alarmed passer-by rushed inside, grabbed teacher Mrs Martin and her pupils, pulled them out into the street where they watched their school fall down before their eyes. The reason for the collapse was that the landlord of the Boot and Slipper had decided his cellar needed extending, and his excavations took him underneath the school's small foundations, with calamitous results.

In 1840 the ancient inn was pulled down, and the Golden Cock emerged in its stead, also covering the site of the school. Down the side ran Golden Cock Yard, a long, narrow affair of four cottages which was sold, along with the hotel, in 1858 for £2,000 and in 1869 for £3,000. It was in this yard that 140 years ago one of Darlington's earliest theatres started up – in 1953 there was still 'a singing-room behind the inn' – and it was from this yard in 1882 that a manure-merchant operated.

Below: The Queen's Head with the bay windows, 1890s . Left: The same view today

The second listed building is another pub: the Queen's Head. Dating from the 18th Century, the Queen's became a coaching house in 1829. Red Rover and Courier called regularly on the London to Newcastle route for several years.

In 1841 the landlord was John Chisman who was the Overseer of Highways for Darlington Borough. An impressive title which he lived up to by deciding that Tubwell Row's 'slope was inconveniently steep and its pavement in an execrable condition'. In other words it was very muddy. He had it reshaped and cobbled – a feature which lasted until 1897 when the cobbles were removed and the slope 'macadamised' with two or three steps.

By rationalising the slope, Chisman made the Row wider and so there was room for the sheep market to re-site from Prebend Row and Bondgate. Poles were erected to which the sheep pens could be tied, and early this century, when the market had run its course, these poles were dismantled

Joseph Thornton's drapery business, 1880s

and are now being used – it is said – to support the chain which keeps people from falling in the Skerne along Victoria Embankment.

The eastern neighbour of the Queen's Head was Edward Todhunter. He was a plumber, glazier and tinplate worker who in 1817 amazed the town by producing gas. This was done in his workshop out the back, and huge crowds gathered at night to watch in astonishment the novel gas light burning in his window. To the east again of Todhunter was the Wheat Sheaf Inn which in 1850 became Joseph Thornton's drapery business.

But all of these buildings, including Harrison's Yard, were lost in 1965 when Darlington Building Society bought the row for £106,000. The lot was pulled down and the Society's drab concrete block replaced it – the final act of the Sixties' evil spirit that not even the Cornmill dared tackle.

PREBEND ROW

THERE were some grand-looking homes on Prebend Row before the Cornmill came along. The prebends themselves, though, seem to have largely been absent without leave.

This meant that the vicars of St Cuthbert's Church had to do their work among the flock, and so their positions were gradually eroded. However, their name stuck. For a time in the middle of the last century it was called

Below: Kitching's Corner between Tubwell Row and Prebend Row, in the 1890s. William Watson is in the corner building where Whessoe was founded . Left: the same The corner today.

Sheep Market – before the selling of sheep was switched to Tubwell Row – and a little later became known as Low Flags, but today those who don't fall into the trap of calling it 'High Row' properly call it Prebend Row. **Kitching's Corner** – the junction with Tubwell Row – was bought by Blacketts the builders in 1921 for £14,500 and demolished. Darlington Corporation tossed in a further £200 so the new building, still standing, would be set back from the road.

But Kitching's Corner has two claims to fame. It was here that **King** James I slept a night in 'a little wainscotted room' in 1617. Next morning, he popped his regal head out of the window and inquired of a **passing** native where his royal personage happened it be (it must have been a heavy night before).

'Darnton,' came the reply.

To which the King – possibly still hungover – snorted back: 'More like Darnton i' th' dirt!' He then hurrumphed back to bed.

The next brush with fame for the corner came in 1790 when Quaker William Kitching opened an ironmongery there. Six years later he started a small foundry out the back. William died in 1819 leaving the business to his sons, Alfred and William Jnr. With foresight, William Jnr immersed himself in the Peases' current project involving the iron railway. He even subscribed £400 to the campaign for Parliamentary permission. When the railway went ahead, the foundry flourished.

The first contract was for 15 guineas-worth of nails to fasten the iron chairs to the sleepers. With the opening of the world's first passenger railway in 1825, orders snowballed until in 1831 the Kitchings had to leave the corner. They went to Hopetown and their foundry evolved into Whessoe.

The two shops next door to Kitching's Corner are part of the same building – one had ludicrous mock Tudor beams stuck on it in the 1920s; the other has a mystery medallion on it which may depict a Greek god called Tonides who was, earlier this century, the emblem of a cigar company. This building is said to be more than 200 years old.

Until the Sixties, Tonides' building was neighboured by a three-storey house which played its part in the hubbub of the General Election following the Great Reform Act of 1832. A balcony was especially suspended from its first-floor windows and from here Joseph Pease, prospective Liberal candidate for the newly-created Southern Division of Durham, spoke with great passion to the assembled multitudes.

His floods of oratory worked for Pease became the first Quaker MP to sit in the Commons, although it was said his Parliamentary speeches never recaptured the brilliance of his Prebend Row outpourings.

In Pease's day the house next door was a lowly, elderly construction which was once inhabited by a certain Matthew Muir who emigrated to America, was consigned to a lunatic asylum (justifiably so, according to those that knew him in Prebend Row) where he leaped from an upper window to his death.

His house survived until the late 1880s when it was replaced by a tall, elegant three-storey building. This lasted nearly a century, its last occupants being a shoe shop.

The changing face of Prebend Row. Left: in the 1890s; Below left: in 1951; Below: in 1986 and right in 1995

Next along the line was a splendid three-storey home complete with bay windows, balconies and all sorts of ornate trimmings – complete, that is, until the 1940s when most of its character was negligently shaved off, a desecration that was completed during the Sixties. Freeman, Hardy and Willis traded here from 1902 to 1988, although they never faced the severe trade war that engulfed their predecessor in the 1830s.

This shopkeeper was a York merchant called John Bacon, a tea-dealer. He opened in 1833 in direct competition to George Craddock, also a tea-dealer, on High Row. Dirty tricks soon began.

Darlington was plastered with handbills practically every day for a year, some published by Bacon; others in response by Craddock. All of them viciously drove an enormous tea-chest through today's libel laws. For example, Bacon on Craddock's goods:

'Go to High Row and buy what you expect to be a pound of tea ... you will pay for a packet of vegetable ad-mixtures, mineral adulterations and poisonous compositions of foul abominations.'

And Craddock said of Bacon that his

'spices were disgusting to the palate and nostrils', and that his currants 'swarmed with animated zoology'.

Bacon is accepted as winning the battle with his rapier-sharp wit, but he lost the war. His other concerns collapsed in Whitby forcing him to withdraw from Darlington in 1838, and so Craddock stood alone.

The Freeman, Hardy and Willis shop from where Bacon launched his massive-missile attacks had been converted from a home in 1819 when the last of the Dove family flew their parental nest. Two generations called Christopher Dove were regarded as the most holy, Christian men in town, but then came William Dove.

A Victorian historian recalled: 'Even in boyhood (William) manifested cruel eccentricities which indicated a combination of diseased intellect and depraved disposition.'

Harsh words, or just hindsight? For in the 1850s William deliberately slipped his wife some poison. She died, as did he – although his end came on the scaffold brought about by the hangman's noose.

PRIESTGATE

THE HOME of papers, phones, Penney, pollution, the Co-op and, in the very old days, priests. Since the men of the cloth moved out in the 15th Century when the Church was selling off its property, their street has changed dramatically and the Cornmill incarnation is only the latest in a long line of varieties.

Only four buildings remain on the south side with any real connection to the past: what was the electrical store Fona (the firm closed down in 1995) on the corner with Prebend Row dates from the early 18th Century; the Red Lion is essentially several 18th Century buildings knocked into one after 1870; and the estate agents Alan Ayers is another early 18th Century building which has been bashed about a bit.

The former electrical store was for more than 100 years the home of William Snaith butchers, which closed in 1984. It was this family firm, founded on the other side of the street in 1830, that provided the beasts for the communal ox-roastings of 1897 (Victoria's jubilee), 1902 (for the subscribers to the new hospital) and 1911 (George V's coronation). In 1964 the firm built a 4,000 sq ft meat factory behind its shop front.

The original Red Lion Hotel was much smaller, comprising just the central part of today's building. When on the market in 1870 it was described as 'truly valuable, old-established and well-accustomed'. The ground floor consisted of a spirit bar, commercial room, parlour, tap room and kitchen; there were seven 'excellent' bedrooms upstairs, and out the back was a 'bountiful supply of spring water' and stabling for four horses. The Lion was not the only hostelry on the south side. A couple of doors down had been the Moulders Arms. It ceased trading in February 1888, was reborn as the Victoria which closed in 1908.

Underneath the Cornmill's walkway is Darlington's first proper telephone exchange. Darlington was first connected to the outside world telephonically in 1887 by the Northern District Telephone Company, although there were only three subscribers to the High Row exchange.

In 1890 the company was taken over by the National Telephone Company and moved to Priestgate with 45 subscribers. All calls were connected manually, originally by boys, but as they were prone to play tricks on callers they were replaced by goody-goody girls.

In turn the girls were replaced by automation. This occurred in Darlington when the exchange moved to the Post Office in Crown Street in 1914. Telephone offices remained in Priestgate and the exchange stayed at Crown Street until 1943 when they moved to Bondgate. The current exchange was opened in 1983.

It is believed that one of the initial subscribers was Pease and Co in their mill at the bottom of the road.

This is entirely consistent with the company's interest in communication. Joseph Pease (1799-1872) would start his day by dropping into the Post Office where just two sorters were employed and help them fish out letters for the mill – a half of all Darlington's mail in the 1820s was for Peases' Mill.

For the 20 years from 1880 Peases' Mill ran one of the largest mail order businesses in Britain. In 1890 the Darlington and Stockton Times reported:

General view down Priestgate around 1900. The telephone exchange is beneath the tall poles in the centre of the picture – roughly where the Cornmill's bridge is now

> *'The only firm in Darlington to conduct all their correspondence by means of the Edison Bell commercial phonograph into which letters may be dictated at any rate of speed desired, and transcribed or type-written by anyone after a few days' practice.'*

Beside the telephone exchange was the entrance to a small yard named after William Feetham who owned it from 1780-1813. Later five houses were built there, and in 1851 these contained 36 people, mostly 'half-clad Irish'. There was a pump at one end and a dunghill in the middle. But then Priestgate's proximity to the stinking, open sewer that was the Skerne did not make it an attractive residential proposition.

Inextricably linked to Priestgate was Penny Yard. This major thoroughfare's main entrance was next door to the Lion, but there were others out onto Prebend Row, the tree-lined banks of the Skerne and south through the Pack Horse Inn yard to Tubwell Row. This large yard dated back to 1720, although it didn't acquire a lasting name until early in the 19th Century when Stephen Carlton set up a coach building factory at the river end.

Also in Carlton's Yard was John Wesley Hackworth, son of railway pioneer Timothy. In the 1830s Timothy built at Shildon the first ever locomo-

Left: Looking down Priestgate in 1965. Above: Priestgate 1995

ive for the Russians. All he needed was someone to take it over there and how the Czar how it worked. Who better than his 16-year-old son, JW?

John sailed out to the Baltic and then travelled by sledge to St Petersburg. During that snowy trip his spirit bottles were broken by a hard frost and he had to escape a pack of wolves. From St Petersburg he went to Tsarskoye-Selo where Czar Nicholas was staying in the Imperial Summer Palace. The loco was welcomed by the Russian hierachy with a baptismal ceremony of consecration into the Greek Orthodox Church. JW returned to England sporting a Russian-style beard, which broke 200 years of clean-shaven fashion. The rest of Britain followed him by becoming trendily hirsuite in the 1850s.

Following his father's death JW started his own engine business in Penny Yard. This proved a successful enterprise for in 1859 he patented the Hackworth Radial Valve Gear, such a big hit among the Egyptian cotton producers that JW was able to build a new works at Bank Top in 1865.

What with Hackworth's foundry, Carlton's coachworks, John Kay's smelly candlemaker's and two slaughterhouses, Penny Yard was not conducive to the good health of ordinary residents. In 1849 it was described as one of the worst of the filthy places ...... all its inhabitants being miserably dirty'. All 30 of them, crammed into eight houses, with their pet pigs running freely about.

Carlton went bankrupt in 1855, and in the same year Hackworth was forced out by the Board of Health who considered his constant hammering and smoke a 'nuisance', so conditions improved a little. But not much: an ironworker from the yard called Metcalfe had five children baptised at St Cuthberts in eight years in the 1870s and 1880s. One of his daughters, Sophia, died aged two by drinking from the spout of a boiling kettle while her sister's back was turned.

Working at the Lion end of the yard was Harrison Penney. Born in Dorset and educated in Hitchin, Hertfordshire, he was invited to Darlington in 1849 by the Peases. Their printer had retired, and they were looking for a good Quaker to take over. Penney, 22, stepped in (he was such a good Quaker he refused to print raffle tickets or circus posters), married a Bishop Auckland girl, and began printing in Northgate.

A fire burnt his first premises and he moved into Carlton's Yard, where he built a tall chimney and became the first printer to use steam power. The yard took a misspelling of his name as its own. A fire gutted his premises in 1861. With the help of public donations Harrison rebuilt, but there came another major blow: his patrons, the Stockton and Darlington Railway amalgamated with the North Eastern Railway, and he lost much of his business. He diversified into bookselling, opening up opposite Snaith's before 1870.

In that year back in Penny Yard, in a former shoe-lace factory the first edition of The Northern Echo was printed. That edition on January 1 contained the news that Mrs Penney had just given birth.

But this was not the first flirtation with newspapers. After 1830 a short-lived weekly paper, the North Eastern Independent, had been printed there. For a while, Priestgate was nicknamed Fleet Street, for it also contained local offices of Yorkshire Post, Middlesbrough Gazette and Newcastle Journal.

In 1887, the main street and the yard began evolving in a new direction; four shops and cellars were let to the Priestgate Co-operative and Industrial Society. In 1916, the Darlington Co-op bought William Feetham's Yard and started a process of acquisition, demolition and redevelopment that lasted until 1961 by which time Penney Yard was built over, and most of the south side of the street one large store. All signs of the Co-op have been erased by the emergence of the Cornmill Shopping Centre.

Some things never change in Darlington

1955
1965
1975
1985
1995

Like good old fashioned Service, Quality and Value.
Mill and Volkswagen - Forty years on - and some things never change

MILL VW CENTRE

THE DRIVE FOR BETTER MOTORING

West Auckland Road, Faverdale, Darlington Tel: 01325 353737

OPENING HOURS: Monday to Friday 8.30-7pm. Saturday 8.30am-5.30pm. Sunday 10am

The Alan H. Goodrick Story

When television first came to this area in the early 50's, there was a serious shortage of qualified television service engineers. A young, ambitious Alan H. Goodrick, realising the potential this situation presented, started his own business in 1953 as a freelance television service engineer providing a service to both private and trade customers.

This proved successful until the early 60's when more and more of Alan's private customers were asking him to provide new televisions, audio, electrical items etc . . . so after a spell in Canada and America where he gained experience of colour television (which had not yet started in the UK) . . . Alan opened his first shop at Northallerton in 1966, followed by a shop at Darlington in 1967.

During the last 30 years the business has expanded and progressed to the stage where it is now acknowledged to be the leading independent Television/Audio/Hi-Fi/Electrical business in the area. This in spite of intense competition over the years from national multiple shops and stores, a number of which have recently ceased trading.

1950 Bush 9″ Television
One of the first televisions in Darlington installed in May, 1950 by a young Alan H. Goodrick

. . . Whatever your requirements in Television, Video, Audio, Hi-Fi and Electrical Products . . .

For the very best deal plus superb pre and after sales service from friendly and knowledgable staff

. . . .Go where tens of thousands of highly satisfied customers have been going for years . . .

Go To Goodrick's

Goodricolour
by
Alan H. Goodrick

30 Years of Quality . . . Service and Dedication to complete Customer Satisfaction

**310-314 North Road, Darlington
Telephone:
465822 Sales/Fax - 480261 Service**

1949   **1995**

"For That Special Day"
consult the Professionals

Complete Bridal Parties Welcome
(will open the salon early for Bridal Parties)

Also available: Manicures/Leg Waxing/Eyebrow Shaping/Eyelash Tinting/Ear Piercing

All available by appointment

All staff fully qualified in City & Guilds and Gents Barbering

Ample Car Park Space and Local Bus Routes

Opening
Times
Mon-Thurs
   9 a.m.-5 p.m.
Friday
   9 a.m.-7 p.m.
Saturday
   9 a.m.-4 p.m.

DARRÚNS SALON

166 Thompson Street East, Darlington
Tel. (01325) 361244

TITLED DEEDS

OVER the centuries, Darlington has twice been shamed by its monarch who has coupled its fair and noble name with lusty, illicit sex. Two kings ennobled their mistresses with the grace and favour title of Darlington. But a Victorian historian said they were 'two as mercenary women as ever disgraced a coronet'.

THE BARONESS OF DARLINGTON

ON JANUARY 2, 1686 King James II created his mistress Catherine Sedley the Baroness of Darlington and Countess of Dorchester after a torrid seven year affair. Catherine's father, Sir Charles, was a poet and a rake at Charles II's licentious court, but his lustful ways had rebounded upon him when his only child took up with James, then Duke of York.

Sir Charles forever bore a grudge against the Royal personage who had deflowered his daughter, and Mary Beatrice of Modena was not very happy either – unsurprising, as she was James' wife and Catherine was her dishonourable maid of honour.

When James succeeded to the throne in 1685 the Protestants tried to turn him against the Catholic priests in Mary's entourage by using Catherine's pillow-talk as their mouthpiece.

It was all too much for Queen Mary who decreed that the harlot must leave London. James politely asked Catherine to go. She refused. James tried to bribe her with the title Baroness of Darlington. She refused again, realising the trumped up nature of the honour. When James forced it upon her, Mary exploded with rage. She shouted like a tragic Shakespearean heroine: 'Let me go! You have made your woman a countess; make her a queen! Put my crown on her head! Let me hide myself in some convent where I may never more see her!'

Left: Catherine Sedley who was created Countess of Darlington by James II, abovve, in 1686

James resolved to banish the new Baroness of Darlington, but being a coward he couldn't bring himself to tell her face to face.

So he wrote to her: 'I know too well the power which you have over me. I have not the strength of mind to keep my resolution if I see you.' He concluded his letter by ordering her to France on pain of her annual £4,000 pocket money being stopped.

Catherine refused. She replied: 'I will not carry my shame among strangers. I would rather be pulled to pieces by four horses than consent to be parted from you.'

The offer of a large slice of Ireland did the trick, but the Baroness of Darlington's banishment didn't last long. She was soon back sharing James' London bed, but Queen Mary accepted her as she had no longer had political influence.

Perhaps Mary was mystified by the hold the harlot had over her husband. Catherine was. She once said to her retinue: 'I wonder why he (James) keeps us; it cannot be our beauty, for he must see that we have none; and it cannot be our wit, for if we have any, he has not enough to find it out.'

'Her form was lean but stately, her countenance haggard,' a contemporary said of Catherine. She loved to dress up magnificently for the theatre, covering her hands with rings, painting her face and wearing Brussels lace adorned with glittering diamonds.

James' elder brother, Charles II, could not see the attraction. He said she was so ugly the priests must have recommended her to his brother as a form of penance. The affair finished when James fled England in 1688 to escape the invading army of William and Mary. Ironically, William of Orange's Mary was James' eldest legitimate daughter.

As the foreign forces swamped the capital, Catherine's father Sir Charles rejoiced. He explained his happiness in terms of revenge: 'I hate ingratitude, and as His Majesty has done me the unlooked for honour of making my daughter a countess, I cannot do less in return than endeavour to make his daughter a queen.'

The Baroness of Darlington went on to marry twice, having two children by each of her husbands to go with the two she provided for James. Her hard-won title died with her early in the 18th Century.

THE COUNTESS OF DARLINGTON

THE House of Hanover was no better. On April 10, 1722 George I bestowed upon the head of his mistress Sophia Charlotte Meisenberg the titles Baroness of Brentford and Countess of Darlington. Sophia's nickname at court was 'the Elephant and Castle' because of her size. Like Catherine, she was intelligent and witty, and although she had extravagant tastes she kept her coffers full by accepting gifts from those who thought she had sway over the king. But she was fat. Horace Walpole wrote:

> *'Two fierce black eyes, large and rolling, beneath two lofty arched eyebrows; two acres of cheeks spread with crimson; an ocean of neck that overflowed, and was not distinguished from the lower part of her body; and no part restrained by stays. No wonder that a child dreaded such an ogress.'*

After some profligate sexual dalliances in her youth, Sophia had jumped aboard the gravy train to England with other German nobility to gather rich pickings in the corrupt English court. For some reason George I took a fancy to her. She had one son by him and later went on to marry Viscount Howe and had another son, later to be Admiral Lord Howe.

When the Countess died in the middle of the 17th Century, Darlington had no name-bearing nobility for a century.

THE EARL OF DARLINGTON

LONG before the Baroness or Countess of Darlington were warming the kings' sheets, the seeds were sown that created the Earl of Darlington. On February 12, 1632 Sir Henry Vane bought Raby Castle and much of Teesdale from the Crown for £9,904 11s 3d to be paid over 35 years. Sir Henry was a distinguished politician who was secretary of state to Charles I and was knighted by James I in 1611.

The first Vane occupier of Raby had eight sons and five daughters. He was succeeded by his eldest son, Henry, who was knighted by Charles I in 1640. Poet John Milton says in a sonnet of this Sir Henry that his 'fame speaks trumpet-tongued to the hearts of Englishmen'.

One of Oliver Cromwell's more famous quotes, though, is less complimentary: 'O Sir Harry Vane, Sir Harry Vane, the Lord deliver me from Sir Harry Vane.'

But it was Charles II who delivered the country from Sir Henry who had become a big name in politics. So big, in fact, that Charles decided 'certaynly he is too dangerous a man to lett live, if we can honestly put him out of the way'. Whether Charles succeeded honestly is a matter for conjecture, but the second Sir Henry walked to the block on June 14, 1662. A conveniently placed band of drummers struck up just as he started the long walk so any last shouts he may have had were drowned out. This suggests a certain lack of honesty, perhaps.

The second Sir Henry went one better than his father having eight sons and six daughters. The eldest three sons died in infancy, and he was to be succeeded by the fourth, Thomas.

On June 21, 1675, Thomas was elected MP for County Durham, but was immediately afflicted with smallpox. He 'was in a fever at Raby upon the day of his election, whereby he died the fourth day after, June 25th, in the morning'. He was 23. The second Sir Henry was followed by Christopher, who stepped into Thomas' shoes as local MP. He had less than five years in the Commons as he was defeated at the elections of 1679 and 1680. However, he must have made an impression: he was created Baron Barnard of Barnard Castle on July 8, 1699.

Christopher would have taken the title of Raby, but it was in someone else's family. He died on October 28, 1723, aged 70.

Christopher only managed eight children, four of each, and relations between father and one son seem to have been a little strained. In 1714 Lord Barnard took some great displeasure against his son who was residing

in Raby and so sent 200 workmen over for a couple of days. They stripped the castle of £3,000-worth of lead, iron, glass, doors and boards. The Court of Chancery adjudicated in the dispute, placed an injunction on Christopher and ordered that he should pay for the castle's reinstatement.

Christopher's youngest son, William, was created Viscount Vane but election to the Commons proved fatal for him as within three days of being returned as MP for Kent he died of apoplexy.

Gilbert, Christopher's third and only surviving son, took over and managed six sons and three daughters – the eldest of which was another Henry.

Raby Castle and Sir Henry Vane the younger who was beheaded by Charles II

This Henry took the degree of Vane nobility higher when on April 3, 1754, the new Prime Minister, the Duke of Newcastle, made him Viscount Barnard and Earl of Darlington. This first Earl of Darlington held high official position, although Horace Walpole attacked him in the House of Lords saying: 'Harry Vane, who never said a false thing, or did a bad one.'

Sir Henry died on March 6, 1758, having married Grace Fitzroy, Charles II's granddaughter who was an heiress to her brother, the second Duke of Cleveland. The Duke was a keen huntsman and was a regular at Raby during the season. One day he was out in the Piercebridge area when his horse came a cropper. To get full view of the action around him the Duke mounted a haystack. This did not go down too well with the farmer's wife who in a loud, shrill voice, called him off.

'My good woman, I am the Duke,' was his reply, but this only added fuel to the old dragon's fury. 'I don't care whether ye be duke or drake, ye shall come down,' she stormed.

Sir Harry and Grace had six children, three sons and three daughters. Two of the sons, Frederick and Raby Vane, were MPs for County Durham, although Frederick only held the position for nine days in 1761. Fortunately for him, though, his loss of seat was not due to his loss of life. Sir Harry's oldest son was Henry, the second Earl of Darlington. He died on September 8, 1792, 'a sincere and pious Christian'. A commoner once visited Raby Castle during Henry's tenure and said it 'presented a warmer picture of ancient hospitality than ever witnessed, or might perhaps ever see again'.

Henry's one surviving child was William Harry who was created a Marquis in 1827 and Duke of Cleveland in 1833.

Many Darlingtonians might think that this historical background has no bearing on their lives. But then their addresses may well be Duke Street or Vane Terrace, Raby Street or Cleveland Avenue, Terrace and Street – all named after the family that once owned the land.

THE DUKE OF DARLINGTON AND THE RAJAH OF CHUTNEYPORE

THIS is a cruel tale of how a simple man who believed he was a weather prophet was fooled into believing he had been honoured with the titles of the Duke of Darlington and the Rajah of Chutneypore.

His name was Thomas Williamson and the first scrape with fame for this Darlington-bred character was in October 1869 when he was signalman at Kelloe Bank, near Hartlepool. The passenger train from Bishop Auckland to Durham collided with some runaway coal trucks from Brancepeth Colliery in front of his signalbox. Thomas noted in his memoirs: 'When the trucks and train did meet they threw the engine over on her broadside, and two poor men under the engine, and of course both were killed.'

He suffered another sad, but accidental, meeting at his box in September 1874 when aged 65. A woman he had earlier noticed dodging trains on the track strode into his cabin and said: 'I am tired of being a housekeeper and I heard tell that you wanted a wife to take care of you in your old age.' Tommy's first wife had died in 1872 after 34 years of wedded bliss. Not romantically inclined, he replied to this strange woman's strange proposal: 'This is not a fit place to have any talk about sweethearting or love or courtship, and particularly when I am on duty, to have any foolish talk on the subject.'

Teetotal Tommy unceremoniously kicked her out, but arranged to see her again. This second meeting led to marriage at Ferryhill Church. The reception was held at the happy couple's new home in Bishop Auckland.

'After dinner and tea were over,' says Tommy in his memoirs, 'I did see some drink brought into the house, but I very soon put a stop to it. But my new wife spoke up and said: 'I am the master of the house now.' So I soon found out that I had done wrong to get married, which it was the case.' He unceremoniously kicked her out for the second time and within three weeks had had the marriage anulled. He moved back to Darlington and devoted himself to weather forecasting, basing his predictions on home-made homilies.

Lord Thomas Williamson, Duke of Darlington and Rajah of Chutneypore

People asked him to predict the weather for their social functions. Usually he replied that it would be fair. If it turned out nice he would turn up and accept their congratulations; if it wasn't he'd stay at home.

His fame spread. On January 1, 1891, he received a letter purporting to be from the Queen. It told him to attend Darlington Police Court where the mayor would ennoble him Lord Thomas Williamson, Duke of Darlington.

Tommy trolled up to the court, presented his letter from the Queen, and even though the mayor burst into laughter, Tommy went home believing he was now a peer of the realm.

An even greater honour was bestowed upon him in February 1892. This time the letter purported to come from India. It read:

'*To the great and mighty seer Lord Thomas Williamson, reader of the stars, foreteller of future events, director of the weather. O great and mighty prophet, condescend but for a moment to peruse this the epistle of thy abject slave, the grand visier to His Imperial and Sacred Majesty the Great Mogul. The fame of your Lordship's weather prophecies having spread even to the dominion of the Great Mogul, His High Mightiness, as a token of his admiration of your wonderful prophetic powers, has commanded me to ask if you will accept the enclosed lakh of rupees. He has also been previously pleased to bestow upon you the governorship of the Province of Chutneypore, in virtue of which you are hereby authorised to assume the style and title of Rajah of Chutneypore.'*

The lack of the promised 'lakh of rupees' didn't stop Tommy taking the enclosed, sealed citation to the court as instructed where once again he handed it to the mayor. Bemused, Alderman Barron opened the seal and read the folowing note:

'Having reached the venerable age of 83 I feel that the time is approaching when...I shall have to leave you for that happier country where the weather glass always stands at 'set fair'. Some of the great men in Darlington have decided, when my time comes, to have me stuffed. They wish still to be able to gaze with love and admiration on my familiar lineaments, and to point me out to their children as the celebrated weather prophet who by his great gifts in foretelling the weather beforehand, rose from being a plough man to the proud position of peer of the realm. My application is that you will kindly allow me to be placed in a glass case near to Pease's monument in front of the King's Head Hotel.'

The envelope also contained a taxidermist's estimate for the task:

'Stuffing His Lordship £1 1s 0d.
Soaking His Lordship's hide in tan pits, 14 days £1 15s 0d.
Boy for frightening the birds off His Lordship when hung up to dry 2/3d.
Scraping, sandpapering and varnishing His Lordship 10/6d.
Barber for shaving His Lordship and cutting his toe nails 1/-.
One strong cork 1d.
Total £3 9s 10d.'

Once again, the court dissolved into hysterics, but Lord Thomas left believing he was Duke of Darlington and Rajah of Chutneypore. He even proceeded to Bulmer's Stone where he posed for some publicity pictures. He died in Eskdale Street aged 86 in 1895. Rather than being stuffed and mounted in High Row he was buried in West Cemetery.

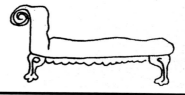

THE MORRITT ARMS HOTEL

Proprietors: Sue Atkinson,
Barbara Anne Johnson

Inn: Close to the famous beauty spot and subject of one of Turner's paintings, The Meeting of the Waters, The Morritt Arms Hotel is itself a famous meeting place. Built where a Roman fort used to stand, the traditional coaching inn dates back to the 17th Century. Staying at "The Morritt" you will capture the essence of a by-gone era. Scott and Dickens both found inspiration for their writings in the area, and are remembered in the names of two of the hotel's bars. Thoughts of Dickens' times are evoked through the genius of the original John Gilroy murals on the walls of the welcoming Dickens Bar.

Restaurant: The elegant oak panelled restaurant is the ideal setting in which to enjoy the finest of British fare. To complement, a range of "New World" wines feature alongside many of the renowned varieties of Europe. You can also enjoy a hearty breakfast, elegant afternoon tea and good real ale.

Greta Bridge,
Rokeby
nr Barnard Castle

The MORRITT ARMS Hotel

Co. Durham
DL12 9SE
Telephone
(01833) 627232

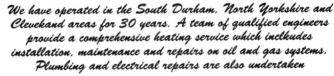

THE WEST END

WEST END FARMS

WELCOME to the edge of town. Salutations. And so a farm got its name. Being a mile or so away from habitation, Salutation also became an inn – its ideal position where roads from all four points of the compass met meant plenty of passing trade.

Salutation Farm dated at least from the 18th Century, but during the second half of the last century, development encroached: first of all West Cemetery ate up lands, then Uplands mansion and finally the Pease homes of Woodburn and Elm Ridge (1867). The farmer gradually turned to dairying.

Until the 1930s this must have been a picturesque corner of Darlington with trees and walls giving the impression of a gentle rural crossroads. Now, of course, there's a roundabout, garage and garden centre. This was done in the name of 'improvement' between 1927 and 1935.

Of course, the demolition of the farmhouse did not mean the demise of its name. Salutation Road is a few yards down Coniscliffe Road and on top of some of the farm's fields. There were once 17 fields stretching from Salutation Corner to Staindrop Road. Cutting through them was the Coal Road, so called because it joined the Auckland turnpike in the north with the Northallerton turnpike in the south enabling the coal to flow from the mines.

All 150 acres of these fields belonged to Salutation Farm's neighbour, Hill Close House Farm which stood on the side of the highest 'peak' in Darlington (over 200ft above sea level) – a hillside that was later to provide nearby Hummersknott with a name (hummer means grassy slope). The farmhouse is today sandwiched between the 1970s' estates of Mowden and Hummersknott, and even though it has had all 17 fields snatched from it, it can still boast that it's the oldest non-religious building in town.

Early in the 1600s it belonged to the Emersons; 100 years later it had been bought by the Allans of Blackwell Grange. By 1854 it was 'the only Tudor house of stone in the parish', and people marvelled at the thickness

Below: Salutation Corner, November 1913. Left: the same junction today

of its walls. During the 1960s it fell derelict, and in the 1970s was renovated. Another ancient farm was Hill Close's nearest neighbour: Field House, on Nunnery Lane and closer to Coal Road. It dated to earlier than 1650, and like Hill Close, farmers prospered on the fertile land.

When up for sale in 1818, this Field House was 'a commodious mansion, seated in a park-like paddock, relieved by a large sheet of water, and approached by a carriage drive through a thriving plantation'.

Soon after Britain hit troubled financial times and the farmhouse was left empty, until 1830 when 20 Carmelite nuns moved in, redeveloping it and renaming it Mount Carmel Convent. The centre of Field House Farm then shifted from the mansion to the farmhouse opposite on Nunnery Lane which, uncared for, finally disintegrated in the 1970s. By the time the nuns at Carmel had settled down, they had been joined by some more women

Edwin Lucas Pease's Mowden Hall

with strange habits – the Poor Clares, another religious order on the run from France who completed their Abbey in 1858.

The land further to the west of the Coal Road on top of Darlington's highest peak was called Bushel Hill – as a couple of street names in that area recall – because a farmer up there would only sell his produce by the bushel (a dry measure of eight gallons).

For well over a century there was a reservoir there which was drained in 1971 to make a paddling pool for a children's play area.

There was also Bushel Hill Farm which John Beaumont Pease of North Lodge bought in about 1865. He immediately created controversy by closing off an ancient highway which ran from the Staindrop Road junction with

Carmel Road over Coniscliffe Moor into High Coniscliffe at Mill Lane.

To fight JB the Darlington Footpaths and Preservation Society was formed with Edward Wooler of neighbouring Danesmoor a leading light. After ten fruitless years Mr Wooler and other local solicitors cut down the obstructing fences allowing Mr Pease's cattle to run amok in corn fields. JB reassessed his position, apologised and put stiles over the offending fences. But then his son, Edwin Lucas, stirred up the same hornet's nest. He demolished Bushel Hill Farm and replaced it in 1881 with Mowden Hall (now the Education Department offices), building a lodge house on top of the footpath.

John Beaumont Pease

The Footpath Preservation Society wouldn't let it lie, and took EL to the highest court in the land. They lost, despite Mr Wooler's representations, and so today's footpath to High Coniscliffe follows a more circuitous route.

Edwin Lucas was an industrialist (founder of Skerne Ironworks), a mayor (1875-6) and keen horseman. The latter was his undoing. At an early age he worked for the family Pease and Partners business.

> *'He was riding home one day when his horse bolted in Northgate and threw him opposite the Kings Head,'*

recalled the Darlington and Stockton Times.

> *'He alighted on his head; the result was concussion of the brain and for some time his life was despaired of.'*

He didn't learn. In January 1889 he was out with the hunt, riding from Piercebridge to West Auckland on 'a high metalled animal with a hard mouth, and its continual pulling tired his rider very much'. On the journey home 'as a ploughed field was being crossed at a good round pace, Alderman Pease's horse fell and almost immediately rolled over on his unfortunate rider'. EL was carried to Mowden (the hall's name is taken from the Mowden Stell which ran nearby) on a mattress and there, aged 51, he died.

THE MINI-MANSIONS OF CARMEL ROAD

HIDDEN behind lines of dark, protective trees in the depths of Darlington's West End are a number of fine large houses that are a legacy of a past opulent era. They cling to their anonymity, displaying burglar alarms far more prominently than name-boards, and the occupants eye suspiciously characters who poke their heads through the foliage 'to get a better look at the architecture, madam' – as much a comment on society as on the author's criminal dress sense.

When Queen Victoria first pulled on her mourning garb, Carmel Road was home to cows and countryside. Today just crossing the road requires a youthful degree of athleticism and a modicum of luck as the cars and artics go speeding by.

More than 130 years ago the Quakers were cluttering up Darlington's arterial roads with their vast mansions and tree-lined parks, so those successful people in the second social echelon were forced to look elsewhere to build their rural 'wannabe' stately homes. These solicitors, bank managers, estate agents, teachers and businessmen chose Carmel Road North, and during the 1860s built a series of impressive homes there and gave them impressive names: Earls Villa, Danesmoor, Osborne House, Greystones, Thornbeck Hill and The Mount.

Sadly much of these houses' histories seems lost. Indeed of the 14 standing on this desirable stretch in 1891, five (Holmwood, Osborne House, The Red House, The Mount and Thorn Lea) are definitely lost for good.

THORNFIELD

THE first of the batch, this was built in 1859 by John S Marley, a mining and civil engineer who was very important in the development of Cleveland's heavy industry. There were stables, coach-houses and pleasure-grounds adorning Thornfield's territory which measured precisely seven acres two roods and 27 perches (however big that might be). The mansion had a strong room and seven servants' bedrooms and it still stands splendidly at the centre of the circular Thornfield Road.

THORNBECK HOUSE

TUCKED away on the Woodland Road corner, this was built early in the 1860s for a Mr TC Shepherd; Thorn Lea was built in 1869; and during the 1870s and 1880s Thornbeck Hill (an ancient name for the area as a whole) was the home of Darlington's most prolific architect, GG Hoskins (the library, the Sixth Form College, the Technical College to name just three).

DANESMOOR

NOW a nursing home, Danesmoor was built a couple of fields south of Milbank Road in 1886 for the lawyer, alderman and historian Edward Wooler. It was noted for its elaborate ironwork, strange sundial and massive central heating system. Conservative Wooler – who held a seat on the council for 30 productive years thanks to election slogans like 'Wooler the Watchdog' and 'Vote for Wooler and Wallop' – was taken ill in July 1927 having just presented the council with the health and sanitary committee minutes. Five hours later, back at Danesmoor he expired, aged 77.

CLEVELAND COLLEGE

BUT not all of these grand buildings were meant to be lived in by single families. Several, like Cleveland College (or St Joseph's Orphanage) at the top of Milbank Road were purpose-built schools. Cleveland College was built in 1869 for Henry Brooks. He took 'a limited number of young gentlemen', according to adverts placed in the Darlington and Stockton Times in 1874 (when he ran the Cleveland Collegiate School) and 1875 (by which time he'd renamed it to plain Cleveland College).

The adverts continued:

'His aim is to impart a thoroughly good commercial and classical education; to cultivate gentlemanly habits; and to combine these advantages with the comforts of a Christian home.'

He had four resident masters – one a 'foreigner' to teach German, French and Music – and the college, 'specially built for scholastic purposes', was set in one-and-three-quarter acres of land. 'The situation,' concluded the advert, 'is elevated, extremely pleasant and salubrious'.

Brooks, a director of the North of England School Furnishing Company, died on March 18 1897 aged 70. But his school had closed ten years earlier, a victim of the advent of the new Grammar School which stole most of its pupils.

In 1893 the Roman Catholic Church took over the premises and converted them into a home for orphaned girls, although the rise on which the building sat was by this time known as Boy's Hill (now Boyes Hill).

The Catholics called it St Joseph's School and ran it for 78 years. Then they changed their policy, preferring smaller more intimate units for deprived girls – like the home they built in Cleveland Terrace – so the 60 inhabitants were moved out. Originally planning permission was granted to turn St Joseph's into flats, but in 1972 it was demolished.

WEST GROVE VILLA

NOW two private residences on the opposite side of Carmel Road, West Grove Villa was a girls' boarding school. It had two large dormitories instead of bedrooms. Facing West Grove Villa was The Mount, another girls' boarder which closed in 1934 and now Highbury Road goes over it.

Private schooling must have been profitable as Thornbeck House became the Collegiate School for Young Ladies in 1870. When its spinster owners died in 1922 it was bought by Darlington Education Committee.

Just over the road, Westholme (now flats called Fairfield) became a boarding and day school around the same time. All are fine period homes, built to be admired as status symbols. However understandable, it's rather a shame that many are now cloaked in secrecy and veiled from view.

THE WONDERS OF WOODLAND ROAD

THIS was once another typically Darlington road, populated by mini-mansions built on paddocks. It is also one of the most controversial of all the town's roads: does it have an 's' on the end of it?

Answer: No, not really. In 1869 the owners of the newly-built villas approached Darlington Town Council Streets Committee and said they were not happy with their street being called Cockerton Road (or Lane). Instead they suggested Woodland Road – perhaps in deference to Joseph Whitwell Pease's spectacular mansion, Woodlands, which was featured in the first Echo Memories book – but even before the last century was finished, maps were being produced carrying the dreaded 's'.

The Woodland Road villa-building concentrated on the stretch from Hollyhurst Road down to Holy Trinity Church. Sadly, most of the houses were demolished around 1963, but tantalisingly the old stone walls remain with bricked up gateways to large disappeared houses.

William Harding

HOLLYHURST

BUILT next door to Pierremont in the middle of the last century, Hollyhurst was originally called Belle Rose and was the home for many years of George Allison, a Quaker lawyer. In the 1880s it was taken over by William Harding, a bachelor stockbroker, councillor and John Pease's private secretary. He substantially enlarged the villa, changed its name to Hollyhurst and became famed locally for his splendid chrysanthemums. Harding died in 1910, leaving an estate worth £102,000. It remained a private residence until after the Second World War when it became a home for the elderly.

BRANSON HOUSE

THIS was one of the very first villas in this part of Darlington before the end of the 1840s. One of its first occupants was James Peel whose name probably does not ring any bells, but he is said to have been one of the best English landscape painters of the late 19th Century. His works fetch up to £1,000 each today.

The artist was born in Newcastle in July 1811. After an unsuccessful attempt to make it big in London he moved into Branson in the late 1840s and left Darlington in 1857 to return to the capital where he did make his name. There are examples of his work in the Victoria and Albert Museum. He died in Reading in 1906. While in Darlington it is believed he worked for Thomas Blyth who was also a painter, only of houses. In 1849 Peel married his boss's daughter, Sarah Martha, who died in 1853 during childbirth. Mother and daughter are buried in Holy Trinity churchyard. The following year Thomas Blyth joined them in the same enclosure.

Thomas's claim to fame is that he was the first president of the Darlington Quoits Club in August 1846. (The club is one of the oldest in the country.) He also won the Silver Quoit competition in 1847.

The Quoits Club's inaugural meeting was in the Dun Cow Inn and their first pitch was behind the Central Hall. Then they moved into the Green Tree Fields off Skinnergate before alighting at Branson House, the home of James Peel. Perhaps he was doing his employer a favour or perhaps he was genuinely interested in the game, but the artist definitely gained inspiration by allowing the players to camp out in his front garden. In 1856 he painted The Quoit Players of Darlington (a fairly imaginative title for Peel who usually went no further than Landscape with Two Cows and Cowman, or, more simply, Borrowdale) which appears to have been last up for sale shortly after his death when it was lost to Darlington. The town's Art Gallery owns eight of his works including Landscape With Shepherd and Sheep, and Landscape with Fisherman.

Quite how long The Quoits Club stayed at Branson House is difficult to say, but their new landlord complained in 1863 about the bad language used by their Richmond opponents. In June 1896, the club bought their current premises in Raby Terrace for £100.

This is not the end of Branson's connection with sport for in 1947 'old men's marbles' moved in. Darlington Woodland Bowling Club bought the house and grounds for £2,500 and is still there.

UPPER THORPE

PROBABLY constructed in 1868 by Quaker William Cudworth – 'designed and built by himself to his complete satisfaction' – who was born in High Row in 1815. However, other sources suggest the building was named after a street in Manchester where the first owner came from. After the Second World War Bishop's School moved in – this clerical school was founded in 1930 in Coniscliffe Road by Helen Bishop (died 1960) who ran it with her brother Walter (died 1970). Upperthorpe Secretarial College closed in December 1991 and the building was sold.

ELMHURST

IT ceased to be a private residence around the time of the Second World War when it became a home for midwives. Demolished in 1963 to allow the Memorial Hospital to expand. For the last year of its life it was a convalescent home for mentally ill patients.

ELMBANK

THIS private residence was bought for £4,000 in February 1926 by the Darlington Queen's Nurses Association. The Association, set up in 1892, provided accommodation for nurses. Its previous base had been in Northgate. Elmbank was demolished in 1963 to make way for more nurses' accommodation, this time for the Memorial Hospital.

THE VICARAGE

PROPERLY know as The Parsonage. Designed and built in 1866 by JP Pritchett for the vicar of Holy Trinity Church. Demolished in 1963 for the hospital extension. Its blocked up gateway can still be seen opposite Milbank Road. A new vicarage was built in Milbank Road.

FAIRFIELD HOUSE

IN May 1918, Fairfield House was put on the market. This caused quite a stir in Darlington's educational circles as for several months the newly-established nursery in Corporation Road had been seeking new premises. This nursery, opened in 1916, was only the third in the country catering for pre-school children, and had been set up as a place where pupil-teachers from the North of England College for Training Mistresses for Elementary School – now the Arts Centre in Vane Terrace – could try out their new skills.

Fairfield fitted the nursery's requirements perfectly, but councillors on the education committee were all away on holiday and so unable to untie the necessary purse strings. The headmistress turned to Joseph Malaby Dent, a Darlington lad born in the Britannia in Archer Street who had gone to make his fortune in the book business in London. His firm JM Dent still survives. Joseph, a keen educationalist with links with the British and Foreign School Society, agreed to loan the money for Fairfield until the councillors returned. In recognition of his assistance, the school was named after his father, George.

Below: Fairfield House which in 1918 was bought and turned into George Dent Nursery School, left

THE ELMS

PROBABLY built in the 1860s, the whole 17 acre estate was bought in 1919 for £30,000. Donations from the Red Cross and St John's Society accounted for half the price, the rest came from workmen's weekly contributions. Financial struggles ensued, but the Memorial Hospital's foundation stone was laid in June 1926, and the wards were opened in December 1932. The Elms villa clung on until demolition in 1930, although specimens from its large, tree-lined grounds still remain, most notably a pear tree in the children's play area and a rare, primitive ginko tree, which must have been imported from its native Japan, in the car park

KILLY-CAT HALL, GREEN BANK AND MAUDE STREET

WEST Lodge, the home of the industrialist Sir David Dale which still stands in the centre of West Crescent, was featured in the first Memories of Darlington book.

West Lodge Gatehouse in the snow. The gates are to the left of the house; Maude Street to the right

Its gatehouse did not. The gatehouse's distinctive oval shape appears on an 1856 map of the town centre. The metal gate beside the house opened onto a long, crooked carriageway which led up to West Lodge. It was on these gates that the locals pinned banners proclaiming West Lodge to be Killy-Cat Hall.

The late 18th Century Lodge was owned by Thomas Backhouse from 1798. He was commonly known as 'Merican due to his times in the colonies and, surprisingly for a Quaker, he had a passion for huntin' shootin' and fishin'. 'Merican also had a nature-lovin' streak and cherished and nourished a colony of rooks and a large hop of wild rabbits.

But the rabbits were 'open to frequent onslaughts by feline marauders' and so Thomas devised numerous devious traps which successfully culled the cat-crusaders. But his neighbours started complaining that all their moggies were getting mangled, and to make their protests heard pinned banners on the gates bearing the legend: 'This is the road to Killy-Cat Hall'.

West Lodge Gatehouse is now at the heart of a quaint-looking office with a verandah on the corner of Maude Street. One hundred years ago this street was nothing more than a dirt track shared by West Lodge and Green Bank Villa. On the track's west side was the West Lodge boundary wall; on its east side were trees and a thorn hedge.

At the top was a large market garden called Spring Gardens, and an ornate footman's house called Swiss Cottage. Built in 1831, the cottage was demolished in 1974 so that the Memorial Hospital could expand.

And then there was Green Bank, which was the first of Darlington's villas to succumb when in 1884 it was replaced by Greenbank Hospital.

During the 1820s and 1830s, Warren Maude lived in Green Bank. A Gateshead man of independent means, both his Christian name and surname live on as street names.

General view up Woodland Road, 1890, including the mural fountain at the Milbank Road junction

MILBANK ROAD

THIS was once on the outskirts of town. Beyond the stone wall there was little but rolling fields and pastures dotted with the occasional farm or rural mansion. Today it is Milbank Road in the heart of the West End. Even round 1900, Milbank Road was farmland, until the Earl of Darlington put the For Sale sign up. 'This freehold building land for sale in lots to suit purchasers. Apply to JP Pritchett, architect and surveyor, 24 High Row.' (Mr Pritchett designed what is now the Arts Centre.)

The stone boundary of Woodlands Villa disappeared into the distance down one side of Milbank Road, and it is easy to see what historian Longstaffe meant when he wrote in his 1854 book:

> *'The only but avoidable drawbacks to the beauty which the approaches to Darlington assume from the snug homes of its magnates, are the long ranges of wall bounding road. These are bald enough but, near a town, what could be done?'*

Apart from St Joseph's Orphanage on the corner of Carmel Road, the only building in Milbank Road was St Cuthbert's Glebe Farm. It was demolished just before the First World War. Why this road should have taken the name Milbank is rather a mystery, as it does not seem to have ever been associated with a mill.

Top: Milbank Road, 1900. St Cuthbert's Glebe Farm in middle distance. The wall to the right still stands. Above left: Looking towards town down Milbank Road. Holy Trinity Church is in the background. Right: The same two scenes today

In the very early days of the last century it was called Thornton's Lonin, quite why is again something of a mystery. Milbank may have been chosen out of deference to a family of former landowners, the Milbankes, who bought a lot of land in Darlington in 1700.

Their most famous member was Sir Ralph Milbank, colonel of the Darlington Volunteers, whose only son died in Hong Kong in 1843 where he was serving as first lieutenant on HMS Childers. There is a memorial to him in the north aisle of St Cuthbert's Church.

Equally, it could be in appreciation of Mark Milbanke of Bedale who married Lord Barnard's third daughter, Augusta-Henrietta, in 1817. Or it could refer to the Milbank buried in nearby Holy Trinity churchyard. Or perhaps it was something entirely different ....

CONISCLIFFE ROAD

MOUNT PLEASANT

A QUICK stroll from Milbank Road through Stanhope Park and Road and out onto Mount Pleasant which is the official name of the first part of Coniscliffe Road. The most famous resident of Mount Pleasant lived in the most famous building: the curved corner house which turns into Cleveland Terrace. He was Samuel Tuke Richardson who, for 30 of his 57 years, was a 'confidential clerk' at Backhouses Bank in High Row. But it is as an artist that he is best remembered. In 1870s-80s he had three sketch books published depicting the Darlington Quakers and the horses and hounds of the local countryside. He was also something of a poet, but it is his sense of satirical humour that shines through.

His most famous work hangs in Backhouses Bank on High Row. It shows Jonathan Backhouse balancing the cash – and his three-wheeled postchaise – on the mad dash back from London when the enraged Duke of Cleveland threatened to break the bank.

For much of his life, Sam seems to have lived above the bank. However, for at least a decade during his most productive period he lived on the curved corner. He retired to Piercebridge where he died in 1904.

He married Eleanor late in life and perhaps this forced him to leave the Quaker faith – he is buried in the village's Anglican churchyard. But at his funeral many leaders of both the Quaker and country sets were present.

Nearly all of Mount Pleasant dates from around the 1820s except, confusingly, what is now called 'Mount Pleasant' – the early 1960s block of flats.

Below: Mount Pleasant, Coniscliffe Road, in 1947. Left: The same stretch today

These flats replaced a run of six houses built in 1822. By 1939, they were ivy-covered and elderly, but still in a solid condition. Then the council bought them. It had some vague road-widening idea, and Mount Pleasant jutted out into the street.

The council allowed the houses to run down. By 1960 it had a dilemma: either spend thousands on renovations or thousands on demolition. When the Ministry of Transport offered a £14,000 grant if the road-widening scheme went ahead, the council took the money and pulled the houses down. By 1964, Coniscliffe Road was wider and the flats – which are totally out of place and bear no relevance to their surroundings – were standing. Many of the surviving homes lost their hedge-lined front gardens and now stand on the pavement.

GREEN PARK

THE Grassy banks of Green Park have for centuries formed a natural theatre for the people of Darlington – even though the Park was not formally open to the public until 1960.

The Park, which is quietly tucked away between Coniscliffe Road, Oakdene Avenue and Harewood Hill, was once upon a time known as South Winter Close. Joseph Pease of Southend (now the Grange Hotel) became owner of the Close some time after 1826.

His estate was built upon at the turn of the century but somehow, as Oakdene and Southend Avenues grew up around it, Green Park remained a natural oasis.

It passed into the ownership of the Waldy family who, from 1870-1901, fell so deeply in love with the view of the Park from the six terraced houses facing it, that they bought the whole row.

This early 19th Century terrace – confusingly known as Green Park as well – appears sturdy but unassuming from Coniscliffe Road. It was designed to look over the Park, and from that side the houses are crammed with interesting arches, extensions and conservatories.

The head of the Waldy family was Dr John, a consulting surgeon. He continued to allow church services and theatre performances to be held in his private park, with the crowd sitting on the grassy banks. Towards the end of his life, Dr Waldy was struck down by rheumatism. Rather than be housebound, he bought a wicker cart and attached it to a donkey which grazed in Green Park. The donkey even had its own 'house' near the Harewood Hill entrance.

Dr Waldy died in 1937. His £60,000 will left many generous bequests to family, friends and churches. It said that once the bequests had been paid, if there was enough money remaining Green Park could go to the town corporation. If not, the prime building land would have to be sold.

The accountants fretted for many months, but Dr Waldy's affairs fell a few hundred pounds short. However, the corporation offered to pay the necessary £598 16s/5d and the three acres of Green Park – plus the famed Tubwell Torrentor fountain – became public property.

BELLE VUE

THIS lovely large villa was built early in the last century and is now the offices of a multi-million pound firm. It first comes to prominence around the 1860s when it was owned by John Hardcastle Bowman. He began life as an apprentice in the leather trade in 1820. 'It was part of his duty after locking up at seven o'clock to be at the workshop before six to see candles lighted,' said his Darlington and Stockton Times obituary in 1898.

Bowman became a travelling leather salesman and he always recalled one 1832 journey – when entering into the North-East hinterland he protected himself with a blunderbuss.

Belle Vue, now No 140 Coniscliffe Road and the offices of Ropners

'He had left Darlington on horseback, well armed, and traversed the district of Durham, Sunderland and Shields, passed Jarrow Slake where he saw the remains of a murderer hanging on the gibbet chains. It was a gruesome sight at seven in the evening, but he rode on, learning by the way that several people had died in Newcastle of cholera. On arriving there he was seized with the dread complaint and believed he should have died had it not been for brandy. Next morning, still very ill, on the strength of more brandy, he mounted and slowly rode for Darlington.'

Bowman's day truly was another age. His name lives on, for with his brother he set up tanneries in Archer Street – the name of the street being a schoolboy pun on his own Bowman. JH Bowman died at Belle Vue in 1898 aged 92, having given fine service to his town on numerous boards. The house was empty for a couple of years before Sir Thomas Putnam took over. When his father William Putnam died in 1897, Thomas (he was knighted in 1918) took over as chairman of Darlington Forge on Albert Hill – a position his father had held since 1860.

Sir Thomas, a racehorse owner as well as an industrialist, renamed Belle Vue Greylands. He died in the house in 1936, and during the Second World War it was used by the military before being taken over in 1946 by Ropners.

This family company, which still has its HQ at No 140 Coniscliffe Road, began in West Hartlepool as a shipping concern. In 1888 it bought the first iron-shipbuilding yard on the Tees and by 1904, with Robert Ropner's patented trunk steamer of 1894, was the sixth largest shipbuilder in Britain.

However, shipbuilding came to an end after the First World War. Ropners remained shipowners and during the Second World War its sizeable fleet was called 'Ropner's little navy' in recognition of the daring way it defied the German submarines.

The company moved to Darlington from Sedgefield after hostilities ceased so it could be nearer the railway line. Since the mid-1960s it has moved into engineering, insurance, garden equipment and property. In the 1990s, this 'mini-conglomerate' concentrated on shipping (it owns two vessels) and property, and from Belle Vue in 1993 made a £3.9m profit.

GREEN CROFT

OVER Cleveland Parade (now called Cleveland Avenue) and past a couple of delightful late-Victorian mini-mansions, is the site of Green Croft. Every Darlington street worth its salt has to have a Pease residence, and this is Coniscliffe Road's.

Joseph of Southend built Green Croft in the 1860s for his sons Gurney and Edward. It was a lofty, Gothic semi in the Pease's buff brick with red sandstone trimmings and plenty of mock towers, triangular gables and a host of rooftop iron twiddly bits.

Edward (1834-80) was the elder brother. Outside the family's business concerns, he was interested in education. He was instrumental in setting up a women's teacher training college (first in Grange Road and then in what is now the Arts Centre in Vane Terrace) and establishing the grammar school. When he died in Switzerland he left £10,000 to found the Edward Pease Library in Crown Street.

His brother, Gurney (1839-72), died even younger. The Darlington and Stockton Times noted rather cruelly in its obituary of the 33-year-old: 'Viewed from the public stand point his life was singularly uneventful and therefore it demands but brief notice at our hands.'

With the brothers dead their vast property – both East and West Green Croft had nine bedrooms – was divided into three. West Green Croft was demolished in the early-Seventies as its twin clung to life while the vandals desecrated it. In 1976, the Anchor Housing Association bought it from the Northumbrian Water Authority and demolished it, building Greencroft Court in its place.

STREETS AND MINI-MANSIONS

TO the south of Coniscliffe Road is the Woodside Estate comprising Hartford, Ravensdale, Woodvale, Woodcrest, Greenmount and Manor Roads.

It was built on the pastureland belonging to the Pease family's Wood Side mansion during the 1920s and 1930s. Hartford Road, for example, was officially named in December 1926 whereas work on Woodside Drive could not commence until the old house it replaced had been demolished around 1933.

On the north side of Coniscliffe Road, hidden by trees, was a collection of luxurious villas and mansions built by Darlington's merchant class. Between Flora Avenue and Elton Parade stood Orchard Croft, so named because it was set in a large spread of fruit trees.

When it was built in the 1850s it was called Flora Cottage which explains the title of the avenue that runs through its old orchards. Elton Parade also bears the name of a large villa: Elton House, which still stands. Dotted around it were Elton Villas, Elton Villa and Elton Cottage.

'Elton Villas have been very recently and most substantially built, are elegant in appearance, having all Plate Glass Windows on three sides, Ornamental Verandahs, handsomely finished inside, supplied with Gas, Hard, Soft and Tees Water, and are in excellent condition throughout,'

extolled an auctioneer in 1865.

But the only one of the smaller Eltons still standing is the Cottage: 'Five bedrooms and bathroom with hot and cold water supply', as an auctioneer's advert boasted in 1899. Of all the comfortable residences in the area Welbeck House stands out, if only because it was designed by GG Hoskins. Now divided into flats, the Elton Parade property was built in 1876 as a girls' training home. It was the philanthropic concern of Mary Anna Hodgkin – grand-daughter of Edward 'Father of the Railways' Pease and so cousin of Edward and Gurney of nearby Green Croft.

Mary Anna (1840-1928) built Welbeck House soon after she was married to bank director Jonathan Backhouse Hodgkin. The school educated young girls so that they would be suitable for domestic service, but as the century turned the demand for maids and servants began to decline and the school was converted into a laundry.

It went under the name of Hygienic Hand Laundry, and a 1913 advert for the business reads:

'In a beautiful open country district. Work of all descriptions done by hand, no chemicals used whatever, and fine linen of

Wood Side Mansion. Demolished in 1930

every kind carefully washed and done up equal to new. All work collected and delivered by van in town and district. Flannel washing a speciality. Noted for the splendid dressing of Shirts and Collars. The Proprietress would be very pleased and esteem it a favour if intended customers would pay a visit to the Laundry. They would then see the way in which the work is done.'

By the 1950s, the Hygienic Hand Laundry was all washed up and closed down. Welbeck House was converted into flats in 1956 which, over the past few years, have had the distinction of many journalists from The Northern Echo residing in them.

Next up from Elton Parade is Linden Avenue which has another Hoskins work on its corner, The Knoll. The Avenue was laid out in the 1890s over the gardens of The Lindens which was probably built for Henry Maddison (1822-1891) in 1865. His firm was Ord and Maddison, agricultural engineers and quarry owners in Wensleydale, Weardale and Teesdale. On his death, his home and his seat on the board were taken over by his son, William Henry Forster Maddison (1863-1917) who was a renowned inventor in his engineering field – several of his inventions were patented as they refined the complex late-Victorian industrial processes.

The Lindens, with its buff bricks and columned front, was renamed Stone House in 1924 at the end of the Maddison era and has since been split into more manageable wings.

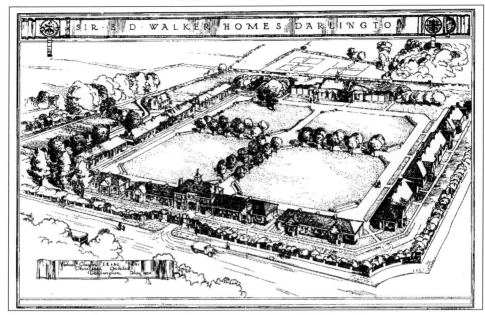

THE ED WALKER HOMES

'A HAVEN of Eventide' stands on the Darlington side of Salutation Corner, dedicated to the memory of a man who was three times mayor of the town. Sir Edward Daniel Walker was born on June 3, 1844 in Brighton.

For 200 years his family had sailed the seas and Brighton was a nautical accident of a birthplace. Soon his father moved north to patrol the wild Yorkshire coast.

ED first came into contact with his adopted town when, at the tender age of 13, he landed a job with the Stockton and Darlington Railway. He worked his way up through station management and telegraphic communications until, aged 35, he saw his window of opportunity.

He baled out of the company and took over the lease on the North Eastern Railway's station bookshops and advertising hoardings. He soon founded ED Walker and Wilson which grew into one of the country's largest provincial newspaper distributors. From 1895-1903 he was involved with the other end of the newspaper business, being the proprietor of The Northern Echo.

Edward – a rose and cricket lover – was immersed in municipal matters throughout his life in Darlington. He was mayor in 1887, 1892 and 1901-2

Above: Sir Edward Daniel Walker. Left: the ED Walker Homes which opened in 1928. Right above: The gatehouse in 1955 and, below, today. Can you spot the differences?

(the first man in borough history to be first citizen three times) and was knighted by Edward VII in 1908.

The peerage didn't matter, though, for across the town he was already known as the 'Grand Old Man of Darlington'. He died on May 21, 1919, leaving much of his fortune as a bequest to build some homes for the aged.

A nine-and-a-half acre site, owned by the Peases, on Salutation Corner was chosen for the venture. To the traditional Georgian design of architect Joshua Clayton, local builders R Blackett and Son constructed 36 homes and 150-capacity Assembly Hall all with 'an airy, lightsome and healthful atmosphere'. A 'special feature' of the homes was an electric bell-push which connected each bathroom to the nurse-matron's house.

This 'haven of Eventide' was opened on June 2, 1928.

The sylvan view down Grange Road in 1890 – the Friends' houses were growing behind the walls

GRANGE ROAD

'THE leading families of the Friends have made their fortunes with their own right hands, and have settled down in all the best and snuggest mansions near the town,' wrote the famed Darlington historian, William Longstaffe, in 1854. 'They love ample gardens and green plantations, plain houses and high walls, and there is an air of the quintessence of comfort in their grounds.'

There is no better example of what Longstaffe was talking about than Grange Road. As the Victorian left the middle class homes of town centre Grange Road, he would have passed the small, two-storey Wellington Cottage which now has the Wellington Court Mews shopping alley built around it. Then came Wellington House, set back from the road a little. It is today the Grange House office block with a new facade – however, it is possible to sneak round the back and see the original tell-tale detailed brickwork. This area of Darlington is properly known as Wellington Place, perhaps inspired by the Duke of Wellington's visit in September 1827 when the villa-building craze was just beginning.

Wellington House had large ornamental gardens, through which a track ran – a track that grew into Victoria Road. In the 1870s, on the far side of

Below: 1890: Wellington Cottage and House in the distance, Orwell House is next to the Baptist Church which is partially obscured by a large monkey puzzle tree in the grounds of Grange House. Left: The same scene today

the track, Orwell House was built. From 1924 to its demolition in 1976, it was a hotel – but it had to go because the track was expanding into a dual carriageway.

In 1871, Grange Road Baptist Church was built at the top of verdant fields that rolled gently down to the Skerne. These fields were dotted with smaller, pretty cottages, each with a luxuriously laid-out garden. These were the homes of second-string merchants and men of industry who did not presume to rival the uncomplicated grandeur of the leading Pease and Backhouse families.

The first villa proper that a strolling Victorian would have come across when leaving the town centre was Grange House.

'The edifice is bold and commanding – retiring from the main road at a pleasant distance. Its suburban locality renders it salubrious, quiet and pleasant, embracing fine views of the

Skerne Valley and surrounding landscape, as well as the more distant compass of the Cleveland Hills; and at the same time the presence of the conveniences which a near proximity to the town is capable of affording,'

gushed the auctioneers' blurb when Grange House was up for sale in 1865. Its gardens and nursery stretched right to the cricket ground – a site that was suitable for it to be converted into a garage in the 1940s and, when demolished in 1991, large enough to send supermarket chains rushing for their cheque books.

Beside it was another mansion that in late-1994 was pulled down to make way for the supermarket. A Backhouse home, Beechwood was taken over by industry in 1932 when the United bus company located its headquarters there. United started in Lowestoft in 1912 and a few months later opened up a run from Bishop Auckland to Durham. The managing director commented in 1920:

The wisdom of the policy of running the majority of buses in coal mining areas, where the population is large and prosperous, is becoming more and more apparent, while the company is enabled during the summer to get remunerative holiday traffic on its East Anglian routes.'

United boomed, carrying a staggering 116,773,356 passengers in 1938. When war broke out in 1939, it was in charge of ensuring the daily transportation of 17,000 workers to the vitally-important Aycliffe munitions factory. Then British Northern Command ordered it to have 250 vehicles and drivers on constant stand-by to help the Army should Northumberland, County Durham and the North Riding of Yorkshire be invaded.

As the war wore on, part of United's depot at Beechwood was set aside for the production of aircraft parts and the assembly of U.S. military vehicles. No wonder Hitler was worried. On May 6, 1942 in Berlin a book was published of objektbilder (target pictures). These included Beechwood and United – although the pictures displayed had been stolen from a 1934 issue of Coach and Bus magazine.

The Germans' booklet was stamped Nur fur den Dientsgebrauch! (For official purposes only!), but it was probably just propaganda. It would certainly have put the wind up Darlingtonians if they'd known one of their villas was on the hit list.

Beechwood was reduced to rubble in 1994 when United moved its headquarters to Yarm Road and Safeway moved in. The supermarket covers

CB 2, BB 6, Nr. 22: Automobil-Reparaturwerkstätte in Darlington (Durham).
"United Automobile Services Ltd." Oben: Außenansicht der Garage und Werkstättengebäude.
Unten: Halle für Großkraftfahrzeuge.

Hilter's objektbilder of Beechwood, the HQ of United Bus Co which was essential to Britain's war effort

Beechwood's extensive gardens which, like its neighbours Rose Villa and Rose Cottage, included hot houses full of the exotica which became all the rage with the 1851 Great Exhibition at Crystal Palace.

The next villa along was the original which started Darlington's infatuation: Polam Grange (featured in the first Memories book). It is now hidden away behind the paraphernalia of the school, it's lodge house demolished and buried somewhere beneath the car park.

Also well-concealed, this time by a curtain of trees, is Harewood Grove. The Department of the Environment describes it as 'an imposing early-mid 19th Century terrace of Newcastle type houses'. Out of sight up the slight rise is Harewood Hill. A pair of these houses date from the late 18th Century and were to be the start of an elaborate square constructed by a co-operative of merchants. With the Grove on one side, and a proposed lawn in the middle, it would have been an exclusive development. However, the money soon ran out as can be seen by the way the first-built is the most ornate and the rest become less and less elaborate. The lawn in the middle never left the seed packet.

On view at the foot of Harewood Hill is the splendid, tall and pointed white-brick Woodside Terrace. Built in the 1860s, from 1872-5 the first five in the terrace were knocked together to form the Training College for Elementary School Mistresses. Here lived a handful of staff and 50 trainee teachers until they were transferred to the purpose-built College of Education in Vane Terrace – which is now the Arts Centre.

To create Woodside Terrace, part of the heavily-wooded area which stretched as far as Geneva Road (now called Parkside) had to be cleared. The ground behind the terrace rises quite steeply – as the hill up Blackwell Lane shows – and at the top, on a grassy plain level with Harewood Hill, was Wood Side.

This mansion was an early-mid 19th Century affair, which in 1848 came into the ubiquitous Pease family. It was purchased by John Harris, a Quaker railway engineer who had become a cousin of Joseph of Southend through marriage. He added the tower and the 80ft conservatory.

During World War One, Gurney Pease's widow allowed her home to be used as a Red Cross hospital for injured soldiers. After her death, the mansion stood empty and was demolished in the late-Thirties.

Another of Grange Road's gems has also been demolished – Park View, the home of the infamous MP Ignatius Trebitsch Lincoln is beneath the petrol station – but plenty of the houses from the 1870s remain. Notable among them is the one that is now flats with its porch supported by marble columns and, on the opposite side of the road, Ashburn House which is now a mock-Gothic office block.

Predating them all is South Villa. Its name was changed to Neasham House in 1898 (apparently when occupied by the Cookson family from Neasham) and it stands alone, shrouded by dark trees, next to the first entrance to South Park. It was built in the early years of the last century and was home to yet another Pease – Thomas who, as the comparatively modest two storey construction suggests, was a member of the second-string of this famous family.

And so this West End walk ends back on the edge of town.

50 years in 1995

CELEBRATING 50YRS OF MEETING ALL YOUR FLOOR COVERING NEEDS

Darlington's Largest Carpet Warehouse is now offering you a huge and varied selection

Over 500 Stock Carpets, over 50 Stock Vinyls, over a 1000 Remnants, Rugs, over 100 Stock Beds and even Curtains and Care-Chairs

So you can choose with confidence the right product at the right price. All this Plus

- ✦ Free Estimating and Home Selection Service
- ✦ Professional Fitting from our own craftsmen fitters
- ✦ Delivery Service with distance no object
- ✦ We are open 7 days a week with Free Parking
- ✦ Paying couldn't be easier

"BUY NOW - PAY LATER" or "INTEREST FREE CREDIT"

It's not surprising that people have been coming back to BURTS for 50 years for

A BETTER CARPET AT A BETTER PRICE

BURTS
CARPET WAREHOUSE

VALLEY STREET, DARLINGTON
TELEPHONE (01325) 466470

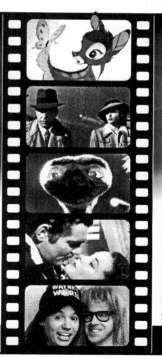

SKINNERGATE

DISASTER struck Darlington swiftly and without mercy on May 7, 1585, between the hours of 12 and one. There took hold 'a most fierce and terrible fire as (if) it had been wildfire, which burned most faire houses in the Towne. It took good holde of pitch, tar, rossen, flax, gunpowder and such like commodities, and ceased not until it had burned 273 houses'.

Much of High Row and Skinnergate were destroyed, which was a catastrophe for in those days High Row and Skinnergate were about half the town. Skinnergate was the western-most edge of Darlington, with fields stretching as far as the eye could see into what is now the suburban West End. It was little more than a back row allowing access to the large, posh houses standing on High Row.

Thatched cottages lined the west side. It never really grew larger than a back alley, but became packed full of tiny yards, filth and disease. And people. In April 1767 a census was carried out. Skinnergate had 148 families living in it, 507 people cramming into 173 houses.

The rest of Darlington was no better. Packed into the 175 houses in Bondgate were 500 people; into the 91 houses of Northgate were 510. People weren't the only things occupying the space. A special census of 1854 showed that 352 pigs made their home in the town centre.

The early inhabitants of Skinnergate were in the leather trade, when that industry was one of the prime sources of employment in the town. So the street got its name, from the Skin Market, that was always held there. In 1621 the local authority ordered:

'Noe tanners shall bye any skins, but upon the Skynnehill.'

But by the start of the 18th Century the leather industry had declined and a sheep market now occupied the time of the Skinnergate merchants. Some of the town's oldest buildings stand in this street. According to the

Skinnergate

Bottom: Looking south down Skinnergate, 1963. Middle: Looking north down Skinnergate, 1936. Left: Skinnergate today

schedule of listed buildings, there are at least ten surviving from the 18th Century.

The oldest of these is probably No 11 (now Le Tiffin restaurant) which includes the archway into British School Yard. It was built around 1700, and here early in the 19th Century lived Dr Peacock who was said to be the last person in town to use a Sedan Chair. As he neared the end of his life he found it more and more difficult to walk, so he was carried into the bedrooms of his sick patients.

Around 1850, when Dr Peacock was no more, Dr Hazelwood moved into No. 12 (Just a Fiver) – a house built around 1750 in which John Wesley is said to have lodged on his last visit to Darlington in 1788. Dr Hazelwood used a different form of transport: he visited his patients on horseback, leaving his beast unattended at their front doors while he attended to them. Never once did the horse abuse its liberty.

The 1822 map of Darlington shows Mr Ord owned the property a couple of doors down from the doctors. About 20 years earlier he had rented it out to a Mr Claxton. 'Depend upon it, Mr Ord, if I take the premises I'll make a paradise of the place,' promised the new tenant. When the landlord turned up unannounced he discovered to his disgust Mr Claxton turned paradise into a cockpit and a pig barracks.

A couple of doors down again was the Cleaver Hotel (now the north end of Argos). It started life as the Chopping Knife Inn at the end of the 16th Century. It was a posting house with a passageway down the side which led to stables out the back. The stagecoach from Newcastle stopped here. By the mid-18th Century it had updated its name to the Cleaver and by 1884 proclaimed itself the Cleaver House Hotel (furnished rooms six shillings a week). It all came crashing down in 1969 when it was demolished.

No. 20 (now Skinnergate News) to the north is a late-18th Century construction, and contains the archway into the Punch Bowl Yard. Today the yard is entered under a sign saying Darlington Finance Ltd. The Punch Bowl pub was at No 21 (the small, curious building occupied by Leggs Stocking Bar) – a late-17th or early-18th Century affair – although it closed towards the end of the last century. The Punch Bowl is first mentioned back in 1630 when it was church property, although the Victorians knew it as either the Royal or, less commonly, the Star.

At about No 23 was the Crown Inn – or the Rose and Crown to those with very long memories – which once stood at the very top of Post House Wynd when that wynd was crooked. The Crown's last landlord, Darnton

The Anchor Inn on the corner of Skinnergate and Duke Street in the 1890s

Guy, left in 1908. Then came the Anchor Inn which was replaced by the Berties building in the 1930s. It wouldn't be fair to give the impression that the Anchor was a tempestuous sort of place, but there are three tales hidden among the dusty back pages of the Darlington and Stockton Times that provide a taste of what it was like.

On August 27, 1852 Supt Robson and a 'posse of police' were called to the Anchor as a gang of between 30 or 40 Irish reapers had hit the Guinness rather too hard, and were now hitting each other. Supt Robson arrived to be threatened by a knife, so he regrouped his posse, armed them with staves and stormed the pub. About a dozen Irishmen were dragged out for a night in the nick, and the following day they were fined between £2 and £10 each.

An early 1882 copy of the paper says Mrs Binks ran into a spot of bother when she was Anchor landlady. 'A respectable young man was fined five shillings for refusing to quit the licensed premises,' records the D and S Times before mentioning that the young man was called George Binks, the son of the landlady.

It may be purely coincidental that a couple of months later when the Anchor reappears in the annals of history the licensee was not Mrs Binks. Her replacement, George Whitfield, was little improvement. In August he was charged with watering down his whiskey, rum and gin so that they were 50pc spirits and 50pc rain.

George didn't attend the hearing himself, but sent his wife who explained that as most people liked a little mixer in their spirits she cut out the water jug and sold the weak liquor direct. The magistrates decided she was simply watering down and fined her 20 shillings. It was no great ignominy – about 20 other town centre pubs faced similar charges that day.

But Skinnergate was one of those places were trouble somehow always seemed to happen. A report in a Darlington and Stockton Times from October 1892's was headlined 'Skinnergate roughs in trouble', and related the latest misdemeanour of 'the notorious McBrides, John and Francis'. The story went:

James Rickaby and family outside his butcher's shop which was next to Burns Yard, 1890-1910

'On Saturday night he, together with his brother, went up to two young men in Skinnergate and asked for a copper. On being refused, he rushed them and knocked them down.'

The McBrides were about to begin some heavy duty violence when lucky PC Muir showed up and hauled the errant brothers off to jail.

The magistrates were obviously fed up with the McBrides: Francis was fined 10s plus costs, and John the ringleader got a 20s fine plus costs plus three months in prison and hard labour. The court's attitude was unsurprising: this was John's 47th appearance.

But enough of the violence: on with the history. Once over Duke Street the next Skinnergate building of note is the former Arcade Cinema (1912-6) – later the Majestic Ballroom and now the Gala Club. Originally this was the Arcade – quiet simply an arcade of shops, built by the Blake family in 1906 on top of the home of Mr Ridsdale and his sisters. Mr Ridsdale was a heckle-maker – a heckle being a comb used in the dressing of flax – and his home had one of the largest gardens in the street.

No. 39, an early-mid 18th Century house, spans Burn's Yard. Originally called Bell's Yard, the name changed early last century to commemorate George Burn, a shoemaker. Over a hundred years ago Mr Burn's neighbours

Left: Fothergill's 1900 picture of where Duke Street meets Skinnergate. The row of houses on Skinnergate were pulled down in the 1920s to make way for Uptons. Right: Today

were the Bowbanks. They owned the Skinnergate mangle, hiring it out for 1d a wring. Their son was Billy, 'a splendid whistler and a well-known attraction at Cockerton Feast'.

And finally came the home of Nut Peter – so called because he ran a nut stall – or Push Cart Peter – so called because he was the last man in town to have a push-cart that was pulled by dogs. He would wrap the poor animals' feet in dirty, bloodstained rags. In the end he was found burnt to death in his Skinnergate cottage – the dogs were not implicated in a revenge killing.

The east side of Skinnergate is blemished by the row of shops directly at the

Tommy Sanderson's umbrella surgery

end of Duke Street. They are on the site of Upton's store, a 1920s-style building, demolished in 1963. In its turn Upton's was built on the site of an 18th Century row of alleyways and houses, one of which was inhabited by Tommy Sanderson, or 'the doctor'. Despite his nickname, he had no medical background. He was an 'umbrella doctor' and his shop universally known as The Hospital For Umbrellas.

Tommy, as well as being an umbrella-surgeon, was famed as a poet, inventor, grocer, publican, bellman and bill-sticker. In 1873 he published a book entitled Chips and Shavings of an old shipwright, or, the life, poems and adventures of Thomas

Skinnergate from the Grange Road end in 1963

Sanderson. Whether Tommy himself ever went to sea is not recorded, but he did live in Sunderland for a while so his antics on the high seas are feasible. He died on September 11, 1890 aged 74.

Moving on from the umbrella hospital, there is No. 74 (now Greenwoods) which dates from around the 1720s, as does the two storey row next to it. The shops between Buckton's Yard and Clark's Yard were built towards the end of the 18th Century.

The Bowes pub is where at the beginning of the 20th Century there were the offices of Messrs Bowes and Sons, wine and spirit merchants. The pub's main claim to fame, though, comes in the mid-1960s when pop superstar Chris Rea played in the cellar bar early in his career. That cellar is supposed to be haunted by a man who hanged himself down there – but he put himself out of his misery long before Mr Rea's performance.

Beside the Bowes is the Mechanics Institute which has been a white elephant for much of its life. In Darlington an Institute was first formed in 1825 with the laudable intention of educating 'rude mechanicals' – anyone who worked with their hands. Books were collected and a library formed, but despite having more than 150 members the Institute was soon wound-up due to lack of interest.

In 1838 it was successfully revived and the meetings were held in Betty's Yard – now Mechanics Yard. As membership grew, so larger rooms were sought: in 1843 it met in Union Street and from 1847 in the Central Hall. On March 14, 1850 it had 341 members and there were 1,367 books in its library. All the big names in the town were represented on its committee: Pease, Backhouse, Mewburn and Dixon.

In 1853 it was decided to move back to Skinnergate and Joshua Sparkes was asked to draw up plans for land which had been bought from the Earl of Beverley. Elizabeth Pease subscribed £400 to the building fund; Mrs Barclay, daughter of John Backhouse, gave £300 and there were many other donations on the basis that the Temperance Society should been able to use the new rooms twice a week.

On May 12, 1853, Miss Pease laid the foundation stone. For her trouble she was presented with a silver trowel in the shape of a fish slice. Weeks later she married and moved to Glasgow and became such a public-spirited lady that she was included in a book called Saintly Lives.

The newspaper room in the Institute opened on April 1, 1854, taking delivery of four daily papers and 12 weekly magazines. On August 25 the rest was formally opened, and Prof Nichol, Miss Pease's new husband, gave a lecture on The Immensity of Creation.

But from the minute it opened the Institute was hampered by debt. In 1855 it organised an exhibition of 'human art and ingenuity' which raised £460. The essay competition was won by a piece entitled 'the victory of Waterloo may yet prove less momentous than the opening of the first Mechanics Institute'.

The 'noble building' was enlarged in 1863 by JP Pritchett, the brother-in-law of John Middleton who built Central Hall and St John's Church, in the middle of its most useful period. When the library (1885) and Technical College (1897) opened, the Mechanics' educational role was largely fulfilled elsewhere and it became a social club.

The Darlington Educational Institute for the Promotion of Science, Literature and Art was due to give the Mechanics a new impetus in 1887, but it proved impossible to raise the necessary £4,000.

On November 23, 1877 two huge plaster casts of Queen Victoria and Prince Albert were unveiled on either side of the platform in the hall. They were removed on utilitarian grounds and destroyed in 1922.

For much of the 20th Century the Mechanics has been on a downward curve. In the mid-1960s it received a coat of paint but it wasn't until the early-1990s that it was refitted as a pub-diner – is this the role this fine building has sought for a century?

Architect Joshua Sparkes has a second work on Skinnergate: the Friends' Meeting House. On August 28, 1678 the Friends had bought a small block of property for the princely sum of £35. This must have been a brave move as during the late 17th Century they were persecuted for their beliefs. Two

Acts of Parliament at the start of the 1660s made their form of worship illegal and in 1684 seven of their number were heavily fined for attending a meeting in a private house in Darlington.

The first Quaker gatherings took place discreetly in the middle of the 17th Century on a farm outside Cockerton where they were less likely to be disturbed. It is believed, though, that their burial ground was in town behind the Black Bull Inn – now known as Humphry's – on the corner of Blackwellgate and Grange Road.

For £35 they bought a cottage with a small paddock behind which became the Friends' burial ground. The wall at the back of the ground is believed to date from the year of purchase which makes it one of the oldest parts of central Darlington. At the start of the 1700s the Quakers bought three neighbouring cottages, and during the middle of the century they pulled all their property down and replaced it with two meeting houses – one for men and a smaller one for women.

In those days everyone had to pay a portion of their income to the established Church of England. The Friends were strongly opposed to this, and throughout the 18th Century they were either sent to prison or had their belongings confiscated and sold by the authorities. In 1825, for example, the Father of the Railways, Edward Pease, had hay worth £28 taken to pay his Church Rates.

The Rev. J Topham, sub-curate at St Cuthbert's, wrote in 1797:

> *I think it is my misfortune to have more of these obstinate people in my parish than in all the rest of the neighbourhood. My predecessor often had the Quakers before the Justices, but this only led to trouble.*

The enlightened reverend said he was prepared to let the matter lie 'rather than live in hostility with them'.

Quakers were staunch in other ways. One day Mr S of Durham was travelling by stagecoach to Darlington when a fellow traveller uttered 'infidel sentiments' and ridiculed the sacred book. 'Friend,' said Mr S who was himself a Friend. 'What do you find so ridiculous in the Bible?'

'What man in his senses can believe,' replied the unbeliever, 'that a stone from a sling could sink into a man's head and kill him.'

'Why,' said Mr S, 'if Goliath's head was as soft as yours there could have been no difficulty about it!'

The first quarter of the 19th Century saw attitudes towards dissenting religions become less hard, although it was not until 1869 that the compul-

Left: Edward Pease's home where Joseph Pease was born beside the Green Tree. Above left: The Green Tree Inn advertising local brewers, Warwick and Co. Above right: The corner today

sory tithe was abolished. This growing tolerance encouraged the Quakers to think about building a meeting house more in keeping with their status as the foremost people in Darlington.

So, in 1839, Joshua Sparkes – himself a Quaker – was employed to design the simple red-brick two-storey meeting house, the only adornment on it being a Tuscan porch. And a tree. Not just any tree, but the Green Tree – a plant with almost celebrity status in Darlington. For centuries it and its successors presided over the Skinnergate corner with Blackwellgate, an inn with fields behind proudly bearing its name.

The first time the tree gets a mention in the town's history is in 1745 when the Duke of Cumberland was marching north to quash the rebellion of Charles the Pretender. The local Quakers believed it would be disastrous if the House of Stuart were restored to the throne, and so allowed 10,000 of Cumberland's troops to camp in the Green Tree fields. The Quaker mills worked overtime to produce a flannel waistcoat free of charge to keep each man warm.

When the news of the victory at Culloden filtered back to Darlington, it is said some of the townswomen were able to boast of the morale-boosting role they played in those nights before the battle.

Beneath the Green Tree's spreading branches lived Darlington's most famous family. A splendid house next door to the Inn was once the home of Rachel and Edward 'Father of the Railways' Pease. John (1797) and Joseph (1799) came into the world here, but soon the blooming Pease family had to move to a bigger home. Their house on Green Tree corner made way for the impressive School Furnishing Company premises in the 1890s. Lloyds Bank is now the occupant.

The tree, though, met its match in the 20th Century when it was decided that traffic was becoming too heavy for such an obstacle to remain. There was great debate about the felling of the tree – that particular specimen was planted on the corner in 1898 and was the third lime to have struggled for life there since 1810 – when the council looked at the matter in March 1924.

'Alas for another disappearing landmark,' bewailed the Spectator column in the Darlington and Stockton Times when the lumberjack's axe had been agreed to. 'Bulmer's Stone lies disconsolate behind the railings of the Technical College and now this tree is to come to an ignominious end by being converted to firewood, that is, if it is worth it.'

By the end of the column, Spectator had convinced himself of the necessity of the operation. 'It is a mere stunted growth that interferes with the ever-increasing traffic of the town,' he trumpeted. 'So down it comes, and that is that.' Opponents of the chop said the Green Tree was the only landmark remaining in the borough.

The tree fell in April 1924 and exactly a year later, the inn which bore its name ceased to trade. Much of the old building was demolished and replaced by two shops owned by the Darlington Model Dairy. In a 1934 advert in the Northern Despatch, the Dairy says it is a 'distributor of Grade A.T.T. Milk and Milk Enriched with Tuberculin'.

The milk trade obviously went sour for the Dairy as it pulled out of the Green Tree Buildings, as they were now called, in 1957. Again there was much rebuilding, and during excavations a one gallon stone spirit jar was unearthed. It bore the legend: 'Geo. Wheatley, wine and spirit merchant, Gainford, 1740.'

There was much excitement as builders thought that the bottle was more than 200 years old, until someone pointed out that 1740 was in fact the maker's number.

Below: Return of the Green Tree in 1965. Left: The same site today

The Green Tree reopened as a 130-seat cafe in September 1957, and then, on the misty autumnal morning of October 20, 1965, The Tree itself made a comeback. Hundreds of years of history lived on until the 1970s when the poor plant again received the chop, but the pedestrianisation scheme of the mid-1990s saw the custom revived.

THE YARDS

POKING off Skinnergate at one time or another have been 19 yards. Although Darlington Council spent at least £60,000 in the 1980s making Clark's, Buckton's and Mechanic's Yards light and pleasant places, packed with shops, the reputation of Skinnergate's yards was unenviable. With an economy of words rarely found in newspapers today, the editor of the Darlington and Stockton Times on January 5, 1884 railed against the despicable quality of the town's yards.

Under the headline Darnton In Th' Dirt, he raged:

> *'I hoped that the appropriateness of the approbrious epithet bestowed on our town by King James had long since become a mere historical joke, and that, with our modern improvements, official grand-motherliness and corporation coddling, all reason for alliteratively associating Darlington with matter in the wrong place had passed away.'*

But the little alleyways and snickleways were proving James right, he said.

> *'The yards are as vile as wet refuse and nastiness can make them.'*

Other authorities were also concerned. Since 1842 the Board of Health had been perturbed about the astronomical death rate in the yards, and in 1899 it ordered that scorriae blocks should be put down in the town centre.

These shiny blue bricks still line many back alleys in Darlington but they are hardly known outside South West Durham. The word scorriae means either 'solidified volcanic lava' or 'refuse from smelted ore'. As South West Durham is not noted for a proliferation of Mount Etnas, it seems likely that these bricks were made out of slag from the steelworks. This would make them cheap, and their shiny quality meant that they could be easily washed down, so removing the dirt and debris that the yards were famous for.

On the down side, though, the blocks were very uneven and became slippery when wet. This is a potted history of the yards of Skinnergate:

BELLS PLACE

Curiously the 1826 map of Darlington shows just a blank plot of land where this cul-de-sac was, even though William 'Hatter' Bell started building work there in 1815. The cul-de-sac fed out into High Row through two yards: Johnson's and Russell's. Hatter Bell owned a shop and house at 35 High Row – presumably he made and sold hats here. Eventually he moved into

THIS is the old Friends Meeting House in 1838, the year before the current one in Skinnergate was built. The artist is JM Sparkes, the son of Joshua who designed the new building as well as the Mechanics Institute.

This picture is remarkable because two versions of it exist, one dated and signed, the other unattributed. The one which bears Sparkes' signature depicts rotten barn doors on the left; hens scratching around the ill-fitting tree protection; a scraggy old man with stooped back and walking stick walls plastered with bills; broke windows, wonky shutters an muddy road and pavement; a d chasing cats down the street and

the largest house in Bells Place. By 1851 there were 11 houses and one lodging house in the Place, inhabited by 50 people, two of whom were officially paupers. Skipping a century, the last person left Bells Place in 1966 when the houses were demolished.

Bells Place – and Skinnergate as a whole – had a proliferation of lodging houses, charging 4d for bed and breakfast at the turn of the century. Due to the transitory and impecunious nature of the people Skinnergate had a reputation as a place not to be after nightfall.

BRITISH SCHOOL YARD

The school was run by the British and Foreign School Society 1819-70, then the Darlington Schools Board took over, transferring the pupils to the newly built Beaumont Street School in the 1880s.

Pupils were taught by the Lancashire system of one schoolmaster and many monitors (the cheapest system) and no religion. Five families lived in the yard in 1884 (the buildings were condemned in 1883). In 1900 the Schools Board held a cookery school there, and in 1909 a shoemaker opened a workshop there.

thing is perfect. The old man is replaced by a dignified couple, the wife wearing a shawl, the gentleman a Quaker top hat. All the doors, shutters and windows are complete and the road is dry and firm. The pesky animals have disappeared and even the sun is out, casting definite shadows. The drunkenly falling man has been replaced by neat and trim mother holding a baby with well-behaved children at her feet.

Which one is artistic licence?

...n lying on the pavement sur-...nded by his possessions having ...t been bodily ejected from one of ...e houses.

In the unsigned picture every-

ANCHOR YARD
Under Duke Street pavement beside Bertie's pub (formerly the Anchor). Had three inhabitants in 1884. Demolished 1890s.

BILLIAM'S YARD
Next to Anchor Yard.

BUCKTON'S YARD
A court in 1882 was told that Buckton's Yard was 'a low slummy place'. Indeed it was the yard with the worst reputation in the whole of Skinnergate. Back in the olden days it was commonly known as Gaping Goose Yard. This nickname derived from the White Swan Inn which had a pub-sign that was so badly painted that the bird looked as if it had a tooth missing.

The White Swan was on the north side of the yard and was a popular haunt of market traders who grilled their own steaks over the bar fire.

The poker, though, had to be kept chained the fireplace because the traders would use anything that came to hand as a weapon if they wished to draw nearer the flames. Such rowdiness caused the Quakers to have the pub closed down in the 1860s – The Grapes Inn down the neighbouring

Mechanics Yard was closed by the nonconformists 30 years earlier for similar unruly reasons.

Buckton's Yard started life as Colling's Yard, due to the family of grocers who bought property there in 1768 when it was the main thoroughfare from Skinnergate to High Row. John Buckton – known as Nancy because of his unusual walk and love of gossip – took over in 1832. He was a director of the Stockton and Darlington Railway and a member of the first Board of Health in 1850. He died in 1850.

One of John's neighbours during the 1840s was Frenchman Joe Raine who had been press-ganged into fighting his countrymen at the Battle of Trafalgar in 1805.

In 1851 59 people lived in ten houses – the late Mr Buckton had moved up-market to Harewood Hill to escape this overcrowding when he became prosperous – and by 1881 there was a brothel there.

The squalor ended when the council closed all the houses in 1900 and gradually the yard became the home of workshops and small businesses.

BURN'S YARD

Formerly Bell's Yard, but changed to honour Geoffrey Burn, shoemaker, around 1850. In 1851 ten people lived there in four houses. The yard has a history of bakery ovens dating back to 1559. In 1900 the Byers family owned the bakery.

Their speciality was roasting Sunday joints from 11.15am. Small, numbered iron spikes were stuck into the joints so diners knew whose was whose. However, if there were four legs in a rabbit pie when it went to the baker's, it usually came out with just two.

CARTER'S YARD

Named after pavior John Carter who lived there in the 1850s. It was also the home of Dick Shaw's bakehouse, Mr Stubbs the picture-framer, and in 1927 William Bryan's slaughterhouse.

CLARK'S YARD

Probably the finest preserved of the three main alleyways. It still has its original 'finkle' or dog-leg, which shows it was once two alleyways – one growing from High Row to Skinnergate; the other growing from Skinnergate to High Row – which collided and became one thoroughfare.

Towards the Skinnergate end of the finkle were the stables where Hussar Troops were put up on their way to the Battle of Culloden in 1745-6. By 1851 James Hunter had taken over the stables and he kept cows there.

The only evidence of a definite date is the drainpipe marked I.P. 1767. This was the side of the house of John Pease which faced High Row and had a long garden (where Boots now stands) in front of it.

John was born on May 13, 1727 in Whitby, the eldest of 21 children. Like his father – also John – he was a grocer, but John Jnr went bankrupt. To compound his troubles the Quakers kicked him out (they said they could no longer be friends) and he retired in ignominy to Ravensworth where he died on December 29, 1794.

John seems to have started building his house in Clark's Yard in the 1750s. Town records say:

> *'1758, William Robson, senior, of Darlington, bricklayer, George Waters, of Darlington, carpenter, both kill'd by the fall of an arch in building a cellar for Mr John Pease.'*

In 1760 John bought the whole of the yard plus one side of Bull Wynd for 400 guineas – an awful lot of money which he calmly carried from Whitby to Darlington in a pouch on the back of his horse.

Following John's downfall the Darlington Herald was printed in his house, and the hoist for hauling up the heavy rolls of newsprint still exists at head-height on the wall. The Herald folded in 1880 whereupon W and T Forster, wine and spirit merchants, moved in from elsewhere in the yard. They built 'a curious wooden erection across the yard, and a wooden gate bearing iron spikes stopped the way to a dozen steps leading down to a dark, damp chamber'.

A corner of Pease's house appears undermined because it was shaped to allow large horse-drawn wagons to negotiate the finkle.

In the middle of the last century, the yard was known as Forster's after the wine and spirit merchants. Indeed, it seems as if in 1830 the Forsters took over the liquor business of the original Clark's in the yard.

But Thomas Clark got the last laugh, for the yard was named after him in the early 1800s and once the Forster's rule came to an end, so their name died and his was resurrected.

The south side of Clark's Yard is incomplete because the rag bag of out buildings in neighbouring Cudworth's Yard were demolished in the 1960s.

Bottom: The entrance to
Newcombe's Yard, 1900. Middle:
Inside Newcombe's Yard: The aisle
of the Court Kinema ran down the
line of the alleyway.
Left: The site was the Court Arcade
and now there is sheltered
housing behind it

CLEAVER YARD

Known in the 16th Century as Chopping Knife Yard before the post house hotel next door was renamed. In 1851 there were three houses in the yard containing 14 people. Demolished 1969.

COFFEY'S YARD

James (Jimmy) Coffey was an active member of the Chartist movement in the 1830s. He was landlord at the Three Bluebells Inn (now the Falchion) in Blackwellgate until hounded out by officialdom and ended up in a small pub at 22 Skinnergate, next door to the Crown Inn and opposite the end of Post House Wynd. Coffey's pub was said to be the quietest in town, where regulars had their own seats and their long-stem pipes were kept behind the bar. Although the pub fronted Skinnergate, the main door was down Coffey's Yard.

NEWCOMBE'S YARD

Where carriers' carts were parked overnight. Skinnergate would have been ideal for itinerant carriers for there were numerous cheap lodging houses, pubs and hotels; and for the horses, stables. The advent of the railway, however, put paid to this form of long-distance travel. The Court Kinema (1914-49) then the Court Arcade were built on its site. In 1994-95, the shops were replaced with sheltered housing.

DOBBIN'S YARD

The alleyway down the side of the old Bainbridge Barker corner store which was built in 1910. Its name comes from veterinary surgeons Dobbin and Taylor who occupied this site from about 1900 to 1910 once the Bellases' Alms houses (built 1636) were demolished.

EDEN'S YARD

Wide entry onto Skinnergate and an iron gate backed out onto the fields which became Duke Street. Demolished 1890s to make way for Duke Street.

MECHANIC'S YARD

Before the Institute opened in 1854 the yard was known as Farmer's (booksellers on High Row) and Betty Hobson's Yard. A ghost – possibly Betty herself – is said to haunt the passage. Until the 1830s The Grapes Inn was a particularly rowdy hostelry, but the Quakers soon put a stop to that and the yard became the home of craftsmen; watch and clockmakers, brass and metal workers, a whitesmith (a worker in tin or a polisher and finisher of metal goods), a bell hanger and a cooper. Alongside these workshops were a number of houses. During the years on either side of the Second World War the complexion of the yard was greatly altered as Binns expanded.

FRIENDS SCHOOL YARD
The day school opened in January 1858 with a classroom for 300 children. Funded by the Quakers. Demolished in the 1960s.

IVY COTTAGE YARD
Where Halford's is now. In 1884 it had four households.

LODGE'S YARD
Named after Lodge Bros the out-fitters which closed in the early Sixties.

PUNCH BOWL YARD
Dates back to the 1630s when it was church property. In 1848 there were 15 Irishmen with typhus lying on straw in two rooms in the yard. A Roman Catholic priest had to break the windows to allow some air in so that he could administer the last rites.

By 1851 there were no Irishmen; but there were 21 other people, including a potter from Barnsley and his family of nine, in five houses. There was also a slaughterhouse which remained there until the 1970s. In the 19th Century 89 inhabitants lost their lives to dysentry. Iannarelli's ice-cream factory opened there in 1965.

SCOLLICK'S YARD
Named after Jonathan Scollick who in 1827 was a flour dealer there. In the 1880s, Frank Long was charged with not keeping his floors washed on a Friday as the by-laws required. In 1891 lodging houses were banned from the yard and in 1902 it was condemned. Probably disappeared in 1930

SUTTON'S YARD
Bought by Darlington Corporation for £755 at the turn of the century. The Medical Officer ordered it should swept and disinfected immediately. In the 1930s it was replaced by what was until 1994 Northern Electric. Named after a family of carriers, three generations of whom drowned.

LOCAL COLOUR

GEORDIE FAWBERT

HE was a lovable rogue. As a council official who had many contretemps with him said: 'He was a worry to us – but we all had a sneaking regard for him.'

George 'Geordie' Fawbert was a cycle shop owner, a mussel merchant, a coal merchant, a fishmonger, a builder, a bus proprietor, a caravan site owner, a property speculator and probably a lot, lot more besides. Apocryphal stories about his intrigues and escapades abound and he became something of a legend – so much so comedians at the Hippodrome made jokes about him.

Geordie Fawbert

He was born in 1874, and made his headquarters in Parkgate. You could tell which house was his because the windows were tied up with string and blocked up with packing cases. It is said that he kept a horse in his front room. One day he complained that the beast made the bedroom directly above smell so someone advised him to open the bedroom window and let some air in. 'I can't do that,' replied Geordie. 'I'll let the pigeons out.'

Geordie was not one of those people obsessed with their appearance. A judge once rebuked him for taking to the witness box covered in soot. Geordie replied that this was the natural state for a chimney sweep. This

Geordie, centre, outside his cycle shop in Crown Street with his father and sister

was not the only time he was up before the beak. One summons was for Geordie the bus proprietor who was accused of waiting too long to pick up a full payload; another was for Geordie the builder for infringing by-laws.

It is difficult to say what his main line of business was, but together they made his fortune, although as he habitually dressed in baggy old trousers, muffler, torn tweed jacket and a flat cap at a jaunty angle who would know?

Once, it was said, he was involved in something of a sock scandal. Dressing for Christmas dinner, Geordie took off his workclothes and climbed into a properly festive suit. Suddenly, he was struck down by a crippling pain in his toe.

After six months of hobbling about, Geordie was all set to go on holiday when someone persuaded him to see a doctor. Holding his nose, the doctor peeled back Geordie's sock – and found a collar stud! Had our hero not changed his underwear for half a year?

G Fawbert's bicycle repair shop was the first in town when he opened it in Crown Street. Like his Parkgate HQ it has since been demolished – it is said that when the Parkgate premises were knocked down in the 1960s a brand new car with just six miles on the clock was found in the yard.

*The 1953 Coronation celebrations in Brunswick Street. Geordie, the barrel-organ
owner, is to the right of the organ; his wife Maude is the large lady to the left*

Geordie bought his mussels from Whitby and sold them on Darlington
market. He bought his fish from Hartlepool, running up there on the train
and bringing them home on the No 24 United bus. Darlington market is tra-
ditionally on a Monday; Geordie saved any unsold fish for Middlesbrough's
Wednesday market by storing it in coal sacks and refrigerating it in the River
Skerne.

This led to a nursery rhyme that was hugely popular among Darlington's
children's in the 1920s-1950s:

> *'Geordie Fawbert, he sells fish,*
> *For three ha'pence it'll make a tasty dish.*
> *But don't buy it, don't buy it,*
> *It smells when you fry it.'*

Using a Model T Ford, he ran the first Darlington to Middleton One Row
bus service. Like passengers on the No 24 from Hartlepool, his customers
had to put up with another Geordie sideline: buckets of coal were stuffed
under the seats.

His caravan sites were on the corner of Valley Street and East Mount
Road and in Archer Street. They were the winter haunt of travelling folk. His
property interests stemmed from an auction at the Imperial Hotel when he

bought seven houses in Four Riggs for £1,000. He paid in cash – he didn't trust banks.

At his side in all this was his wife Maud. She was 25 years his junior and originally his housekeeper. It is said that one morning she awoke with terrible stomach pains. Geordie called a cab and took her to Greenbank Hospital where the doctor examined her and told Geordie he was about to become a dad. 'I'll have to marry her now,' said the proud father.

Indeed it has been suggested that Maud was the brawn and Geordie the business brains. She had a wooden cart onto which she unloaded fish at Bank Top Station and then dragged her cargo into market. At the end of the day she would buy wooden orange and onion crates from James Ward's market stall. She would wheel them home on her now fish-free cart, chop them up, bind them into bundles and sell them as firewood. Maud outlived her husband, as did their daughter Rosemary who moved to Leeds. Geordie died on May 11, 1960 at the grand old age of 86.

ALF COMMON

DARLINGTON has not produced many footballing favourites, and its most famous soccer star is adopted. But what a claim to fame he has!

Alfred Common retired to the town in 1919 after a glittering international soccer career which was not without a hint of scandal but during which he sensationally became the first £1,000 player. Alf was born in 1880 at Millfield near Sunderland, and the Wearsiders were his first big club before a £325 transfer took him to Sheffield United in 1901.

The following year he became the youngest player ever to win a FA Cup winners' medal (a record which has since been eclipsed). In the summer of 1904 Alf returned to Roker Park for a club record fee of £520 (a record which has since been eclipsed). He stayed at Sunderland for seven months.

Fellow First Divisioners Middlesbrough were enduring one of those seasons: rooted near the foot of the table, they had not won away from home for nearly two years. In January 1905 they approached their arch rivals and asked if Common was for sale.

After two months of negotiation, Alf arrived at Ayresome Park, and chalked up a record which can never be eclipsed: he became the first £1,000 footballer. This exorbitant sum was considered scandalous by the whole country. Questions were raised in the House of Commons.

Middlesbrough were portrayed as extravagant young upstarts (the club had only been in the Football League since 1899) and Sunderland were reproached for daring to ask for such a sum.

The Althletic News snorted indignantly:

> 'As a matter of commerce, ten young recruits at £100 a piece might have paid better, and as a matter of sport, the Second Division would be more honourable than retention of places by purchase.'

Harsh words indeed. Presumably the footballing establishment thought Middlesbrough should simply sit back and accept their dismal fate.

They didn't, and the ploy worked. Common's first game for the 'Boro on February 25 was on a ground he had graced earlier in his career: Bramall Lane, home of Sheffield United. United were awarded a pen-

Alf Common in England kit

alty in the first half which was put high over the bar. Three minutes into the second, Boro's winger was tripped in the area, and Alf stepped up and calmly scored. For 42 desperate minutes 'Boro defended stoutly, but held on. Back home 2,000 fans greeted the news of the victory by throwing their hats into the air. The revival continued, and Middlesbrough staved off relegation.

Common was 5ft 8ins tall and weighed 13st. He was an aggressive forward, deceptively quick and 'brawny and full of stamina'. His best season was 1905-06 when he scored 19 goals in 36 appearances.

Alf on the ground having just scored for Middlesbrough against Sunderland on Jan 1 1906

Middlesbrough at the time was a club hot with scandal. They were accused of attempting to bribe opponents into losing so that their chairman would win an election the following day; illegal signing-on payments were made; they were accused of 'trafficking in players'; their books never tallied, and they seemed constantly on the verge of bankruptcy and relegation. Alf himself was stripped of the captaincy and fined £10 in September 1907 for drunkenness and violent behaviour.

In August 1910 the 'Boro were short of cash. Even though Common had returned to the team for the last month of the previous season and kept them up when relegation seemed inevitable, the club chairman offered him a free transfer – providing he didn't claim the £250 benefit money promised to him earlier.

In the interests of the club, he accepted the deal, and moved to Woolwich Arsenal leaving behind him a respectable record of 65 goals in 178 appearances. His career, which included three England caps, had a final honour to come: the Second Division Championship with Preston just before the war.

And so he retired to Darlington and became landlord of the Cleaver Hotel in Skinnergate. Six years later he transferred to the Alma Hotel in Cockerton where he stayed until 1933.

John Prior specially built the Alma for himself in 1860 when he had finished building the street beside it which bears his name. He chose the word 'Alma' to commemorate an 1854 battle fought over a newly-built Russian

Alf in the England line-up, fifth from the left

fortress during the Crimean War. (Coincidentally the town of Alma-Ata now has a population of over a million and is in Kazakhstan.)

For a few years after Prior, the Alma was called the Jubilee Hotel, but from 1878 right through the alterations of 1937 and 1954 it remained the Alma. In January 1969 it was bought by the Whitbread brewery which, ten years later, embarked upon a substantial redevelopment programme and rechristened the pub The Brown Trout 'to bring it more into keeping with Darlington'.

Obviously not in keeping enough, for another decade later it became The Beer Engine. What was wrong with Alma, as it was in Alfie's day? He left the pub game in 1933 having become so devoutly Methodist that he led those congregated in his bar to church.

His retirement came the year after his son, Alfred Jnr, was involved in a motor accident that put paid to a second Common career. Aged 18 at the time, the youngster was on Sunderland's book and said to be even more talented player than his old man.

Alf Snr saw his days out in Coniscliffe Road and died 11 months after his wife on April 3, 1946. As steeped as he was in North-East football, he would not have been surprised to see that his adopted home-town team hasn't progressed beyond the lower reaches of the Football League. Throughout his time in Darlington he maintained that the football club would never succeed while it played at Feethams.

Tasty Treat for children after public ox-roasting

Echo Memories – every Monday

EASTBOURNE AND HUNDENS

GENEVA Road curves elegantly around from Yarm Road roughly following the edge of the fields of Brankin Moor Farm. Then it comes to Neasham Road which travels out to the villages across the moor. Not as desolate and bleak as most moors, it takes its name from the fern plant that grew on it.

It was here that the Battle of the Bracken was fought. From the year dot, the borough of Darlington consisted of the market place, the streets or gates around (although not Bondgate which was a separate village) and three farms a mile or so away on Brankin Moor.

The Moor was supposed to be common pastureland where anyone was allowed to keep animals, although the burgesses (the privileged class) and the more lowly inhabitants often disagreed about how common this common was.

From time immemorial there had been four 'beastgates' on the Moor which were separated from each other by dykes, and these stretches of land were attached to burgesses' houses in Tubwell Row.

Early in the 17th Century the borough decided to appoint a hirdman to keep the animals and their owners in order. The hirdman can't have been a successful peacekeeping force, for soon the borough was employing four grassmen to prevent the battle of the bracken escalating.

A fine of 6s 8d was imposed in 1621 on anyone who 'shall fell the whins (gorse or bracken) and bring them off Branken Moore without the consent of the Grasse men'. Instead of stealing, people were supposed to buy: the grassmen sold bracken and gave the money to the borough.

The ordinary people seemed to have accepted this, for the finger of suspicion points at the rich burgesses who 'willfullie and obstinately' stole the whins. But the reasons why they should have been squabbling over bracken has been lost in the fern fronds of time. The most obvious cause would

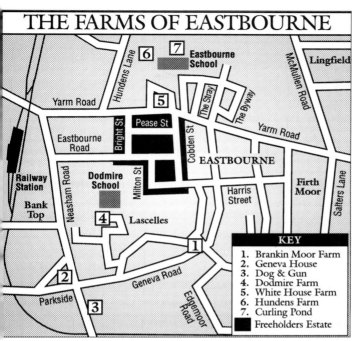

THE FARMS OF EASTBOURNE

Map of the farms of Eastbourne

KEY

1. Brankin Moor Farm
2. Geneva House
3. Dog & Gun
4. Dodmire Farm
5. White House Farm
6. Hundens Farm
7. Curling Pond

Freeholders Estate

have been that the plant was used as a cheap substitute for hay as bedding for horses. However, it is now known that bracken is in fact poisonous to grazing animals like sheep and horses.

Brankin Moor Farm dates back to 1684. Over 100 years ago it was 160 acres in size and the farmer concentrated on dairy herds: he had 127 acres devoted to grass, and the rest to arable. When the farm was sold in 1907, the farmhouse had five first floor bedrooms and four attic rooms above. In the out-buildings there was room for 43 cows.

However, it was not sold for farming. As the estate agent's blurb pointed out, there was a tram terminus outside the farm's front gate on Yarm Road, and to the south of the estate ran the Eaglescliffe branch of the North Eastern Railway: this land was ideal for housing.

And so began the Eastbourne housing estate, so called because it was on the east side of town, with Geneva Road as its main artery – named after the large Geneva House (demolished 1956) where the new road met Neasham Road. Two other farms were gobbled up by Eastbourne. To the south there was the Dog and Gun, another ancient site of habitation. It had been an inn popular with farmers from the outlying villages as they trekked into market.

In 1864 the innkeeper allowed his licence to lapse possibly because improvements to the roads meant the farmers sped by without stopping.

However, the landlord can't have been too keen on custom for he stocked such low quantities of beer that whenever a thirsty farmer called in, he had to get on his horse and gallop off to the nearest pub to get supplies. The Dog and Gun successfully diversified from farming at the start of this century by picking up on the Edwardian equivalent of paintballing. It became a centre for pigeon shooting and rabbit coursing, and by the First World War it had become such a den of iniquity that gamblers came from the pit villages further north. However, the post-war depression ended this sideline and in 1934 the farmhouse wearily succumbed to the developer.

The other farm under Eastbourne is Dodmire, a medieval name still commemorated by the school. One theory is that this land was originally called Dodmans Close which in turn came from the word 'duds' – a pernickety little spirit not dissimilar to Will o' Wisp.

Perhaps it was Will o' Wisp that possessed Dodmire farmer John White who was known as a hard drinker. Some would say an excessive drinker, and this consistent abuse was driving him mad. On the evening of February 14, 1822 he had had one too many once again, and came to the conclusion that his farmhouse was infested by robbers.

All night he strode the house, refusing to turn in, carrying a loaded shotgun with which he promised to blow out the burglars' brains as soon as they had the bottle to show themselves. White had a young servant, John Gales, who was an ordinary sort of lad and didn't suffer alcohol-induced frenzies. At six o'clock the following morning Gales got up, got dressed, and came downstairs to start another day's hard toil.

'Strange,' he thought to himself when he found the back door locked, and returned to the kitchen to find the key.

In the passage outside the deluded farmer heard the noise and knew it was the robbers come at long last to lift everything he owned. In one movement he stormed the kitchen and emptied the contents of his gun into the intruder.

Gales fell to the floor by the fire, clutching the door key. He died two hours later. Farmer White was later found by the coroner's jury to be in a fit of mental derangement at the time of the incident, and was discharged.

The first part of Eastbourne to be developed was the Freeholders Estate of Harris, Cobden, Bright, Pease and Milton Streets – all these bar one are great Liberal Quaker names. The odd one is Harris which comes from John

1906-08 Hundens curling team

Harris, a Quaker engineer, who bought 46 acres of land off Yarm Road in 1851. In those days, to qualify for a vote, you had to own land with a rateable value of £10. Therefore, Harris sold off plots that precisely qualified in the hope that the new electors would vote Liberal.

Over the road from the Freeholders Estate was White House Farm, a small-holding that was developed in 1912-23 as The Mead by the Darlington Garden Suburb Company – a concept of greenery that didn't catch on in Darlington as it did elsewhere in the country.

One farm that escaped the attentions of the builders was Hundens which, like Dodmire, dated back to the 13th Century. Its land has now been taken over by Eastbourne School and the council football pitches, and its connection with sport goes back a long way for here was a sizeable curling pond. Curling was called 'the roaring game' and it was a roaring success in Darlington. Ponds proliferated all over town, and in the winter they were converted into curling rinks. The biggest was the manmade one at Hundens Farm, but also popular with curlers were Polam Pond and Pease's Pond in South Pierremont Gardens, Woodland Road.

Curling is a Scottish game introduced to Darlington by the mid-Victorian economic migrants. One of those was William Maben (1856-1948) who hailed from Gatehouse of Fleet in Dumfrieshire but came south because he couldn't find employment. In Darlington he did, and worked as a Scotch draper – a door-to-door household linen salesman armed with patterns who collected his money in weekly installments.

The Hundens showground in 1920

Darlington Curling Club commenced in January 1879 in the Fleece Hotel, Blackwellgate, during a spell of serious winters. In 1879-80 it was possible to skate along the Tees from Blackwell to Middleton One Row and from Croft to Coniscliffe.

The one problem with outdoor curling is its reliance on the weather – the game against Malton on Pease's Pond in 1879 had to be abandoned half-way through when the thaw started. When warmer winters set in during the 1920s Darlington Curling Club was disbanded. Another factor in the club's demise was the growing interest in bowls.

In summer, Hundens Pond was a mecca for model boaters.

Early this century, Hundens Farm was a mecca for socialites for it was touched by Royalty. More than 182,000 people poured in. And naturally enough, being England in the summertime, it poured down. The farmer's fields turned to mud, and all the heavy machinery got stuck in the mud.

This was the Royal Agricultural Show, one of the premier events of the year in anybody's diary. Its first visit to Darlington was to the beautiful rolling park of Hummeruknott in 1895; its second and last was to this unprepossessing farm midway between Haughton Road and Yarm Road in 1920. Hundens was chosen despite being 130 acres of undulating clay soil with dubious drainage properties (as today's footballers will testify).

Its chief attraction was the proximity of the main railway line, and the North Eastern Railway Company went to the unprecedented lengths of adding three sidings to create the farm's very own depot and station. For in those days the roving show was like a pop star's world tour: it took a year to set up the showground; ten tons of nails, 70 tons of canvas and more than 1,700 tons of wood were used. It kept about 80 men in employment. Darlington town council weighed in by building a new access road: Hundens Lane (and presumably this is where the grand green gates to the sports ground come from).

Pride of place went to the Royal Pavillion, which was a grand five-roomed affair with its own 'old court garden'. The large dining room was oak panelled with carvings and rich hangings. The private retiring room had walls of golden brown leather and a panelled wooden frieze. All the furniture was Jacobean oak, and watercolours adorned the walls.

The man who graced Darlington with his presence was the Duke of York, later King George VI. According to the Darlington and Stockton Times he was 'such a clean cut unassuming English youth, fresh as a May morning, extremely anxious to avoid any fuss and 'jolly glad' when the brief ceremonial was over'.

The crowds flocked to see him. Haughton Road, the paper reported, was 'one solid mass of humanity moving'. The roads all around were choked with 'really amazing motor traffic'. Every restaurant in town was eaten out' and at night South Park came alive with a fantastic firework display. The farmers, though, were probably more impressed with the machinery on display. More than 500 firms exhibited 5,000 new fangled pieces of equipment. The Darlington and Stockton Times remarked: 'The farmer who expressed the opinion that the day was not far distant when he would be able to sit at home and allow the farm to be run by mechanical means was perhaps a little ahead of his time.' But not by much, concluded the paper having seen the array of the technology of the 1920s.

The third day of the show was subject to a 'pitiless downpour' and yet still 56,000 people visited. But the day after the future king and crowds had all gone home, the July weather broke its cheeks and Hundens was awash. All the stunning 1920s' technology was bogged down, along with the Royal Pavillion.

It took six weeks for the Pavillion to be extricated from the Hundens quagmire and despatched to Derby were the 1921 show was to be held – the workmen usually reckoned on this operation taking three weeks.

Below: The Duke of York at the official welcoming in High Row outside the Covered Market.
Left: The Duke and Duchess of York at Hundens

Perhaps the organisers should have been warned. A couple of months before the grand opening, the main entrance buildings were destroyed by gales. The cost to replace them was £1,000, and the Society had been using them every year since 1886.

And perhaps they should have known better than to trust Darlington. In 1895 the Hummersknott showground was struck by an electrical storm that killed two men outright. It also made a hero out of Spider the Horse, who stars in the first Memories book. In 1920 the death was that of a nine-year-old boy from St John's Chapel. He jumped off a tramcar and in his excitement to get into the showground rushed across the road and under the wheels of a car. The car belonged to the Marquis of Londonderry. He was the acting president of the Royal Agricultural Society and was escorting the Duke of York around the site at the time of the accident.

124 YEARS OF QUALITY ZISSLER & SONS

The Founders:
George Christian and Magdelina Regina Zissler

The Present:
Paul Victor and Sue Zissler

For four generations 'The Old Firm' has been manufacturing quality traditional pork products daily at:

104 BONDGATE, DARLINGTON

INDEX